NEVER HOLLER

To all the men, women, and horses who have chased the chuckwagon wind.

CONTENTS

ACKNOWLEDGEMENTS

A heartfelt thank you to Buddy Bensmiller, Jim Nevada, Kelly Sutherland, Troy Dorchester, Mark Sutherland, and their families. Their honesty, sincerity, and willingness to share their unique lives is what makes this book special.

I also thank the competitors, staff, and families within the chuckwagon community; driver Orville Strandquist for inspiring the book's title; editor Sue Sumeraj; Paul and Carol Easton; the enthusiastic public affairs staff of the Calgary Stampede; and especially Arnold Gosewich of Balmur Entertainment.

As well, I thank Dr. Donald B. Smith for his encouragement to write, my two cheerful pals Tony Fiala and Blaine Harasimiuk, my family for their nurturing support, and especially my mom and dad for taking me to my first chuckwagon race.

Finally, my most heartfelt gratitude goes to my wife, Joanne. Years ago during a tender courting moment, she gazed at me and asked, "What's going through your mind?" and I responded, "I'm dreaming of driving a chuckwagon." Amazingly, she stuck with this writing cowboy, and her love sparks this book.

INTRODUCTION

Welcome to Wagon Racing!

Picture yourself in a ready-made coffin tied by tooth-floss to the tails of four charging dinosaurs. That's wagon racing.

MARK SUTHERLAND, CHUCKWAGON DRIVER

It's 7:00 p.m. Just one hour till tonight's first wagon heat. Thirty-six anxious chuckwagon cowboys and their crews are pacing in the barns, calculating which four horses they will hook up. Devising their strategies, they begin to pull the horses' harnesses off the wall. As the leather creaks and the buckles jingle, the attentive horses begin weaving and prancing in their stalls. The adrenaline swells in the barns. It is sixty minutes to High Noon.

To step into the cowboys' world of chuckwagon racing is to ride into the hoofbeat of the West. Every chuckwagon race delivers a rush of excitement. Wagon racing spurs the imagination, conjuring notions of vast prairie vistas, unending blue skies, and charging wild mustangs. Holding the lines to this sport and their way of life are the chuckwagon cowboys. They roar out from under the chinook wind's arch; they are the static behind the wagons' thunder.

Yet the cowboys, heroic in their determination to succeed on the racetrack, define themselves away from the crowds, behind the track. It is in the horse barns that they are at home. Here, the cowboys discover and live chuckwagon racing — these barns hold the soul of the sport.

Within the buildings, the air is pungent with the scent of sweet fresh hay, earthy horse sweat, and the tangy bouquet of Copenhagen chewing tobacco. One glimpses sweat-stained straw cowboy hats; glistening, rippling horse flesh; and children curry-combing horses. Chuckwagon racing is the smooth feel of worn leather; the roughness of slivered pitchfork handles; and the polish of a bronze trophy.

Wagon racing is also the sugary taste of a country fair: cotton candy, candy apples, and mini-donuts; the rich flavour of pancakes and bacon grilled outdoors; and the sweet bite of a rye and Coke — "the champagne of the prairies." It is the sound of creaking wagon wheels; the echoing clip-clop of horseshoes; and the cowboys' eager "Hyaw!'s" and whistled "Shweet-Hah!'s." Chuckwagon racing captures the optimism of summer, the affection of friends, and the undying romance of the West.

The men who indulge in chuckwagons love the sport. Sincere, feisty, and welcoming, they and their families create a unique, mobile community. Their hardiness and hospitality reflect western living and a pioneering spirit that persists today. The men and women are salt of the earth, and they are dedicated to a horse-driven culture filled with dangers and joys.

Cowboy legends tell us that a Texas cattle baron, Charles Goodnight, was responsible for creating the first "chuck wagon." In the 1860s, during the beginnings of western cattle ranching, Goodnight purchased a used Civil War army wagon and fashioned it into a mobile kitchen. Goodnight built a pantry-like box on the back and filled it with the "chuck" — the grub or chow of the cowboys, which included the essential sourdough, coffee, and "whistle berries." He also added a tool box on one side, and a water barrel on the other. A long canvas tarpaulin was pulled out from the wagon to cover the pantry. Meanwhile, harnesses, slickers, and cowboy bedrolls were kept inside the wagon; and under the wagon, a cowhide was slung to hold wood and buffalo chips that the cook collected for fuel.

The camp cook was responsible for driving the wagon horses, preparing three hearty meals a day, and even offering haircuts and shaves. In the evenings, the last chore of this teamster was to point the pole of the wagon toward the North Star, providing a compass heading for the trail boss in the morning.

Often-recounted range stories reveal how much the working cowboys depended upon their cooks. (Cowboys hated cooking.) One tale goes that a particular cow camp had lost its cook and a cowboy reluctantly volunteered, growling, "Alright, I'll cook, but the first man to complain is the new cook." After a week of serving unpalatable food but with no complaints, he decided to end his purgatory by cooking up a meal of prairie cow-pie stew. One cowpoke took a mouthful of stew and proclaimed, "I'll be damned, this tastes just like a cow-pie . . . but, it's good."

The chuckwagons were used throughout North America from the 1860s to the early 1900s, during the heyday of the range cowboy. The chuckwagon became the cowboys' "home on the range." During cattle drives, the camp cook and his chuckwagon drove in front of the herd, joining the trail boss in leading men and cattle across the plains, sometimes for hundreds of miles and for weeks at a time. The versatile chuckwagon teamsters were seen from Texas to Alberta, wherever cattle were herded and cowboys grabbed their eatin' irons.

The early wagon men were not immune to competition and showing off their driving prowess. At Fallon, Montana, in 1892, the cooks from the Hog Eye and L-Cross ranches were in town to stock up on supplies. Before starting back for camp, the teamsters "joined the crowd for a little irrigation," and naturally the cowboys' talk turned to horses. In time, a cowpuncher staked a case of whiskey on the merits of his cook's team of horses.

Cowboy W.H. Peck recounts in the Calgary Herald: "The cooks by this time were fairly well loaded inside, and the wagons were loaded with the camp supplies. It was decided to run the wagons on a six-mile course, and the first wagon back was to take the hootch. Baldy Wright was given the honour of firing the starting gun. When he gave the signal about twenty other guns blazed forth just to make no mistake about the start." Peck adds, "With all the noise and hullabaloo, off they went, neck and neck, horses pitching and lunging, frying pans and Dutch ovens rattling, cowpunchers yelling and shooting to scare the horses; and the bosses looking pretty glum, wondering how the dog-gone thing would end."

The Hog Eye outfit won by one hundred yards. Peck recalls, "The aftermath of the race was felt and tasted by us for at least the next ten days. We had beans, sugar, coffee, and mica axle grease in our grub."

As homesteaders and barbed wire began to crisscross and colonize the plains, the open range was no more. The days of the great cattle drives ended. Yet chuckwagons were still used on western ranches, and wagon teamsters continued in their mainly practical role until 1923.

In 1923, the New York-born Guy Weadick, promoter of the first two Calgary Stampedes in 1912 and 1919, was asked to organize his Wild West celebration annually. To do so, Weadick believed he needed an enduring attraction. With his entertainment savvy, Weadick saw in ranching's heritage an event that would combine the cowboys' swaggering with the electrifying thrills found in ancient Rome's chariot races: organized chuckwagon racing was officially born.

In proposing the world's most unique horse race, Weadick was aided by Alberta rancher Jack Morton. Morton, a tall, powerful, and generous rancher, was nicknamed "Wildhorse Jack" for his inclination to hook wild, unbroken horses to his ranch wagons. The chuckwagon races witnessed on Morton's ranch were similar to those seen all across the West. After a roundup, he and his competitors would race to the nearest ranch house or saloon, and the last teamster to arrive was obliged to buy a round of drinks.

Weadick's early promotions for chuckwagon racing read as follows:

Primitive, rattling, lumbering, range-scarred, mess wagons fully equipped. Their daring drivers on the swaying seats handling the ribbons on the fastest four-horse team their ranch can produce. Old-timers who know no fear, and daredevil young'uns desperately pitting their skill in racing rivalries. They break camp, load their wagons, cut a figure eight around two barrels, and run a half mile on the track to finish under the wire in just under two minutes.

In the first structured chuckwagon races at the Calgary Stampede, after the wagons finished circling the racetrack, the cowboys were required to bring their outfits to a halt at the starting point, unhitch their team, set up a cookstove, and start a fire. In the traditions of the open range, the first outfit to have smoke rising from its stove was declared the winner.

Since no rules prohibited him from doing so, Jack Morton carried a bottle of gasoline to help hasten the required smoke. In his first race, Morton produced an explosion and fire, but little smoke. The blast also caused Morton's horses to detonate. Rearing and lunging, they tried to bolt out of their collars.

At the first Calgary Stampede Rangeland Derby in 1923, the Mosquito Creek Ranch wagon won with the best aggregate time. This meant that after five days of racing, Bill "Sourdough" Somners and his crew had accumulated the lowest combined time. The prize was a new Stetson hat. Somners was over seventy years old, and like the rest of the first competitors, he was an experienced teamster who had honed his skills driving hundreds of horses on Alberta ranches.

The early cowboys were also instrumental in the development of a Calgary tradition: chuckwagon breakfasts. In 1924, Jack Morton trailed a herd of bucking horses into Calgary for the Stampede's rodeo. Once in the city, the range chuckwagon that Morton used to feed his cowboys along the trail was soon serving tourists and Calgarians breakfasts on the downtown streets. The hospitality and friendliness found behind the wagons has been spread from Calgary streets and shared around the globe.

Jack Morton also displayed the persistent toughness that characterizes chuckwagon cowboys. On the second day of racing in 1924, Morton's wagon lost a wheel. Wildhorse Jack was thrown from his seat, dragged by the horses, and broke several ribs. Shrugging off the injuries, he nevertheless drove the next day. A day later, a broken leg resulting from a friendly wrestling match still did not stop him from racing.

Throughout his driving career, Morton was also known to recklessly throw his reins to the ground during a race. Bellowing at his horses to run faster, he counted upon his outriders to catch his horses by their bridles. Morton's western antics were just what Guy Weadick hoped for to ensure swelling spectator curiosity and entrench the frenzied wildness in chuckwagon racing.

The fundamental style of a chuckwagon race has remained the same since the sport's beginnings. The races are run with four competing "outfits." Each outfit consists of the driver, a racing chuckwagon, and four horses pulling the wagon. The horses are paired off: the two horses at the front are called the "leaders," and the two horses closest to the wagon are known as the "wheelers." Four pursuing outriders on their horses follow the wagon throughout the race.

To identify themselves on the track, cowboys and their outriders wear team shirts or jackets bearing similar colours. Today, the outfits competing at the Calgary Stampede wear colours based on barrel position: Barrel 1 — white, Barrel 2 — red, Barrel 3 — black, Barrel 4 — yellow. For many years, the drivers selected their own brightly coloured shirts to match their chuckwagon's colours. Outriders who rode in every heat for different wagons did not have time to change shirts, so they layered the shirts, peeling one off after each race.

In a wagon race, each outfit completes a short figure-eight turn around a set of barrels placed in the infield (the area within the racetrack oval). The cowboys refer to this part of the race as "turning the barrels." Since four teams compete in each race, four sets of two barrels each (eight barrels in total) are positioned on the ground. The barrel positions are numbered 4, 3, 2, 1, from left to right.

Approximate configuration of the Calgary Stampede Rangeland Derby's starting barrel turns

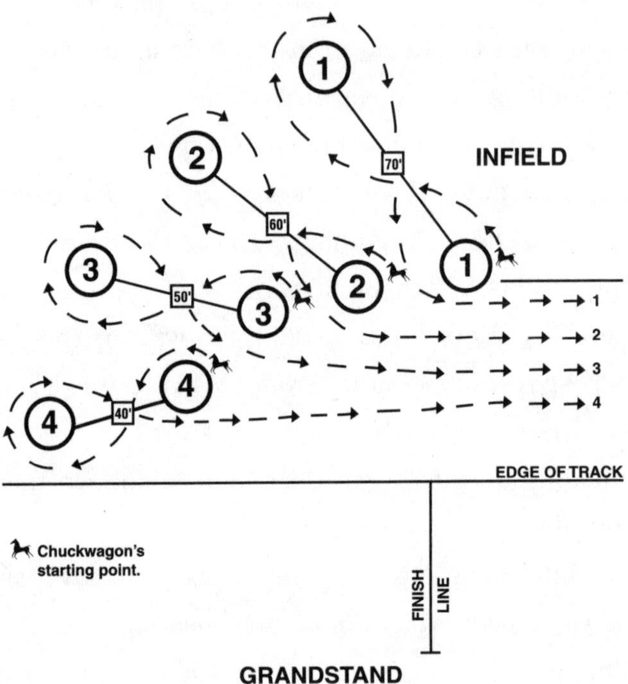

The term "barrels" itself comes from chuckwagon racing's origins. Initially, wooden kegs with steel hoops were used in the competitions. These barrels were a driver's nightmare. If hit, the kegs were heavy enough to flip a wagon; and when smashed, they left unsafe bits of metal and splinters in the dirt. Over the years, the wooden barrels have been replaced by metal drums, then heavy cardboard, and finally now plastic barrels that collapse if touched by a hoof or wheel.

Once the outfits complete their respective figure-eight barrel turns, they face a five-eighth-mile counter-clockwise race around the oval track. Prior to 1925, at the end of the race each team had to unhitch its horses, set up a cookstove, and start a fire — before a winner was decided upon. But to make the races more thrilling for spectators and cowboys alike, this setting up of camp was eliminated in 1925, allowing the outfits to charge neck and neck down the homestretch to a wire finish.

The length of each figure-eight turn is staggered to help make the overall distance the outfits travel equal. For example, the outfit on Barrel 4 must run eighty feet farther around the racetrack. To compensate for this extra distance, at the Calgary Stampede, the space between Barrel 4's two figure-eight barrels is forty feet, compared to seventy feet on Barrel 1. The result is that Barrel 4 is known as the "short barrel," and Barrel 1 as the "long barrel." Proportionately, the space between barrels on Barrel 2 is sixty feet, and on Barrel 3 it is fifty feet. For each set of barrels, the barrel located farthest in the infield and the first barrel turned is the "top barrel," and the second barrel turned is the "bottom barrel."

Barrel 1 has the reputation of being the barrel position a cowboy needs to win. Rounding Barrel 1, the wagon is in the lane leading straight to the rail position — which offers the shortest distance around the track. If all the wagons complete their barrel turns at comparable speeds, the wagon on Barrel 1 will be next to the rail, and the Barrel 4 wagon will be farthest from the rail. Yet although Barrel 1 is the most coveted, it is also the most difficult to turn. Of the four barrels, Barrel 1's exit onto the track is the most sharply angled. The torque created in this hard, tight, left-hand turn results in the greatest odds of the chuckwagon flipping onto its right side. Over the years, the turn off of Barrel 1 is where a multitude of chuckwagon wrecks have occurred.

The most frenzied action of a chuckwagon race takes place at the start. It is also the moment when the four outriders play their most critical roles.

Seconds prior to the starting horn blowing, each wagon slows to an impatient stop to the right of its bottom barrel. The back wheels must not be in front of the bottom barrel or a one-second penalty is assessed. One outrider grabs the leaders, steadying the horses and pointing their heads in the right direction. This outrider also helps to keep the tugs tight. Connected to the singletrees, the tugs are strong leather straps that carry the bulk of the stress from the horses to the wagon. If the tugs are slack at the race's start, they can snap as the horses lunge forward.

At the rear of the chuckwagon, the other three outriders walk up behind the wagon. One bends down to grab the "stove." (Originally, the stoves were heavy camp stoves, but now they are ten-pound rubber simulations.) The two other outriders each grab a five-and-one-half-foot-long tent pole (or tent peg) and stretch out the canvas fly. At the horn, the outriders throw the stove and tent poles into the wagon. Both the stove and the tent pegs must be successfully loaded into the wagon box, or penalties will be assessed to the outfit. The stove must be placed in the low metal rack situated at the wagon's rear, and the tent pegs and canvas must be thrown into the wagon box. The outriders' jobs are a throwback to ranching heritage, representing the cowboys breaking camp on the open range. (At many shows outside Calgary, often only two outriders are used by each outfit: a stove man and an outrider holding the lead horses.)

Once camp is hopefully loaded in the wagon, the outriders lead their balky horses to the top barrel. This ensures both outriders and horses are out of the wagon's path as it rounds the top barrel. Then, without using their stirrups, the outriders jump into their saddles, and now on horseback, they chase their chuckwagon through the figure-eight turn and around the racetrack.

The barrel turns are the key unpredictable factor in chuckwagon racing. Driver Troy Dorchester describes, "You can't really make a strategy in a wagon race 'cause you don't know where the hell you're going to come out around the barrels. You might think you've got your best horses hooked, but you still might be the fourth guy coming around the barrels."

As the race ends, the first outfit to cross the finish line is not necessarily the victor. Numerous judges are situated around the track, monitoring the race. During the race, and afterward through video replay, the judges review the race, looking for and assessing penalties. These penalty seconds are added to the cowboy's "running time" — the time it takes for a cowboy's first lead horse to cross the finish line.

Penalties play a key role in chuckwagon racing. For example, the outriders must try to keep pace with their chuckwagons throughout the race since outriders are considered "late" if they are not within 150 feet of their wagon when the lead team passes the finish line. A late outrider's outfit is assessed a one-second penalty.

While racing, chuckwagon drivers can be seen looking over their shoulders to find their outriders. They try to determine if they need to rein back their team to let a tardy outrider catch up. Since the drivers have the right-of-way on the track, outriders stay to the middle or the outside of the track. Generally, outriding horses bear half the weight of a wagon horse, and can travel quicker;

however, if the outriding horse had a slow barrel turn, an outrider may have to risk riding along the inside rail to catch up.

Altogether, there are more than thirty basic racing penalties to avoid. Some of the most significant infractions and their penalty times include the following: tent pole left dragging (each pole, 1 second); stove not loaded into the wagon before the wagon hits the track (4 seconds); wagon knocking over a barrel (each barrel, 5 seconds); outrider knocking over barrel (each barrel, 2 seconds); and wagon interference (1 second, plus any additional time penalty charged at the judges' discretion). Drivers loathe penalties. Each chuckwagon race is timed to one-hundredth of a second. During a week of racing, mere fractions of a second can separate competitors, and a one-second penalty can cost a driver thousands of dollars in prize money, trophies, and sponsorship.

A chuckwagon "show" consists of two to ten days of races. Presently, the Calgary Stampede hosts a total of thirty-six wagon cowboys contesting all ten days. Each day of the Stampede, all of the cowboys race: that means nine heats of four wagons each. At other smaller shows where the racetracks are narrower, twelve heats with three wagons per heat may be hosted. A wagon will run only once each day. Races are usually held in the evening, following the afternoon rodeo performances. In order to create fair, exciting races, the wagons are pooled in their heats based on their present standings in the circuit (at the season's first show, they are pooled based on the previous year's final standings). The quickest outfits race in the last heats of the day.

During competition, the thirty-six outfits are ranked according to time. An outfit may finish first in its heat, but be ranked fifteenth in the show, due to faster-running outfits competing in other heats. Similarly, an outfit may place third in its heat, but be ranked second overall due to its combined, or aggregate, running time. Throughout the show, the outfit's time from each evening's race is added together until either an aggregate-time winner is declared or, as in the example of the Calgary Stampede, the four overall fastest outfits of the show earn berths in the winner-take-all final heat, which is held on the last evening.

With thirty-two horses and twenty men charging en masse in a race, chuckwagon racing was labelled, not surprisingly, "The Half Mile of Hell." Chuckwagon racing is fundamentally a horse race, but it is no conventional flat race. The event's unequalled appeal lies in the great number of variables compacted into seventy-five seconds. There is constant unpredictability.

Throughout the years, rules and penalties have been continually adapted to make the races more action-packed but also safer. What initially began as an entertainment spectacle has evolved into a regulated sport, complete with standards and rulebooks. One significant rule change was the standardization of racing-wagon weights. At the sport's beginnings, bulky, lumbering ranch wagons were raced. Water barrels hanging on the sides, tools, and even working ranch stoves were all part of the outfit. But there were no weight standards, and heavier, slower wagons sometimes vied against lighter, faster ones.

As of 1943, however, every racing wagon, with its driver on board, had to weigh a minimum of 1,325 pounds. To pass the weight scales, cowboys owning light wagons threw in an extra piece of lumber or a hay bale. Other less-principled drivers gave their wagons a thorough washing, especially on the inside, realizing that their wagon's unpainted wooden boards could soak up forty pounds of water — weight that would evaporate before the evening's race. Restrictions are now strictly enforced to ensure minimum standards are maintained. Today, at the Calgary Stampede, if a wagon inspector finds a light wagon, the driver receives a one-thousand-dollar fine, and a two-second penalty is added to his running time for that evening's race.

Up until 1948, the use of whips was also allowed. The whips were a motivator, making quick horses out of those that were not so fast. Handling four reins in two hands is difficult enough, but when a whip is used, the four lines are held in one hand. It was an intricate challenge to both control the horses and aim the whip. It was not unusual for an innocent outrider to feel a whip wrap around his neck, sending him rolling in the dirt. Outriders learned to keep their face buried in their horse's mane to avoid the whip's searing sting.

The ongoing adaptation of rules and improving equipment have raised the level of safety and reduced injuries for both cowboys and horses. Wagon cowboys are concerned about their horses' safety, often more so than their own. Their horses are their passion — they are members of the cowboys' families. If a horse is hurt, the cowboys immediately tend to the injuries. There is no pleasure in seeing a horse wounded.

Chuckwagon racing today little resembles a mad dash to the nearest saloon. It is a professional sport requiring specific racetracks and equipment. Driver Jim Nevada states, "When we've tried to sell wagon racing in the United States, the organizers haven't realized what is involved. They thought we could just dig a circle in a field and run across the prairie. They didn't realize the sport is just as intense as thoroughbred racing." He continues, "We need a track with the right specifications. The wagons are well taken care of; they even require specific grease. It is not like the old days when you just grabbed an old buggy, made it lighter, and raced. There's an art to the sport."

Professional chuckwagons are capable of racing at forty to forty-five miles per hour. Hot-blooded thoroughbreds, rather than stocky draught horses, now pull the wagons. The wagons are light, and the horses are swift. Nevada notes, "It's only four horsepower, but the power of the horses is just unbelievable. People don't understand the force created until they get into a wagon."

The manic energy produced results in races that are as awesome to hear as they are to see. As the horses, wagons, and men careen around the oval track, the ground positively shakes. It is high velocity, it is unmechanized, and it is raw.

For the three months of competition, the cowboys commit to twelve months of effort. Chuckwagon racing is a year-round undertaking. Contrary to some spectators' beliefs, the cowboys do not simply gather their horses from the pasture five days before the Calgary Stampede and head to town to race. The horses' spring training lasts over two months, and the cowboys always have chores to do in the barns or are calling for medical attention for a horse.

The crux of wagon racing remains the horses. The cowboys' thoughts rarely waver from their racing cohorts. Chuckwagon cowboys live in rural areas in order to accommodate a large stable of wagon horses. The top skinners own forty to sixty thoroughbreds, and they turn over 30 percent of their stock each year. When they are not racing, the cowboys are purchasing, training, and selling new and old horses.

To succeed in this sporting life, professional chuckwagon

cowboys must possess veterinary skills to look after their animals, agricultural skills to manage their farming operations, and commerce and marketing skills to run their chuckwagon operations, which are essentially small businesses. They are prairie renaissance men. Because chuckwagon racing demands such an array of talents, there are only about sixty professional thoroughbred chuckwagon drivers competing in the world, all concentrated on the North American plains.

From June to August, the members of the chuckwagon community load up their motorhomes, trailers, and stock liners, and take to the road. Families drive over 5,000 miles each summer to attend wagon races across the West. The cowboys from both the World Professional Chuckwagon Association (WPCA) and the Canadian Professional Chuckwagon Association (CPCA) follow their circuits of shows.

Most professional chuckwagon races take place in Western Canada, from British Columbia to Manitoba. Races are also common in the United States. Recently the pro wagons raced in Pomona, California; and Kennewick and Moses Lake, Washington. In Wyoming, Cheyenne's Frontier Days also hosted wagon races for half a century.

Slightly different styles of chuckwagon racing have also arisen across the western United States. For example, the Chuckwagon Racers of Iowa-Minnesota Inc. have eight members, who compete at regional country fairs. They began racing around 1965, and today the eight wagon teams identify their wagons and team members with specific colours, such as Orange, Purple, and Gold, and race using taller wagons with wider wheels (four inches). These competitors race strictly as a hobby on a half-mile track, and they follow racing rules similar to those of the pro wagon associations. They also hold a two-wagon Powder Puff Race with female competitors.

Pony chuckwagon and chariot races are also popular in Western Canada. They have even been held in the Houston Astrodome, in Australia, and in South America. In pony races, horses may have thoroughbred stock in their blood, but they must all be shorter than fifty-four inches at the withers. Lighter and smaller chariots and chuckwagons are used by the drivers, and generally, no outriders race in the heats. Pony wagon races offer competitors, including a number of female drivers, the special thrills of chuckwagon racing without the same financial demands found in thoroughbred wagon racing.

The "Super Bowl" for every professional chuckwagon cowboy remains the Calgary Stampede's Rangeland Derby. Any cowboy who has ever dreamed of running a chuckwagon has dreamed of racing at Calgary. The Rangeland Derby culls the world's thirty-six best chuckwagon cowboys and brings them together. Running ten days, the Calgary Stampede is the longest chuckwagon show, the richest and the most gruelling.

No other major rodeo or fair holds chuckwagon races on the scale that Calgary does. Over 25,000 people jam the grandstands and the pampered luxury suites to cheer the races. With Joe Carbury's call — "And they'rrrrrre off!" — the race commences. Television cameras are set around the track to also show the action and replays on a JumboTron screen. The chuckwagon races have become the unrivalled soul of the Calgary Stampede, and above all, they are what makes the Calgary Stampede "The Greatest Outdoor Show on Earth."

Chuckwagon racing remains the only bona fide western Canadian sport, a fact Canadians do not often appreciate. Born in the Alberta foothills, and sustained on the prairies, the races still occur primarily in the Canadian provinces of Saskatchewan and Alberta. The sport has yet to develop the same fans, the same prestige, or the same reputation anywhere else.

Part of the reason why Canadians champion the event rests in the fundamentals of chuckwagon racing and its distinctive culture. To illustrate, spectators might assume that chuckwagon cowboys and rodeo cowboys are cut from the same herd. In fact, there are important differences. Both groups of cowboys celebrate western heritage, but they do so in different ways, which reflect their unique values. For example, in rodeo, the principle of the roughstock events (such as bull riding) is one man versus one animal. The lone cowboy depends upon his own skills, and although cowboy and animal are evaluated together, they are judged based on their individual talents.

In contrast, the essence of wagon racing centres on teamwork. Although the winning driver receives the fame, his victory depends upon the ambitions of a cohesive and well-running team of horses. He also counts on a reliable squad of outriders. No matter how skilled the driver is, if a horse acts independently, or if one outrider makes a mistake, then the whole team can fail.

Most importantly, a family and community effort is needed to maintain, train, and move the number of horses and equipment needed. To compete, a rodeo cowboy can jump into a pickup with his rigging bag and go down the road, but a chuckwagon cowboy travels with a minimum of eight horses, plus feed, tack, a wagon, and a motorhome. Even the barrel-racing cowgirls, who travel with one horse, are much more mobile than wagon cowboys. Many of the cowboys are qualified to drive semi-trailers, in order to haul their outfits to the shows. Family and friends assist in and out of the barns, and their help is necessary just to travel to the racetrack, let alone care for the horses, look after harness and tack, and prepare the horses to race.

The distinctions between wagon cowboys and rodeo cowboys stem from each sport's origin and tradition. The persona of the rodeo cowboy is built on the solitary working cowboys: the men who have relied upon their own abilities to work amongst cattle and horses. Their success was judged on their own skills. The belief in the individual continues to be central to American culture and is reflected in the cowboy mystique. Meanwhile, the chuckwagon cowboy personifies the co-operative spirit of Western Canada. Although the Canadian West was also settled by autonomous individuals, these people developed a society based on British beliefs and convictions. A faith in public responsibility was reflected in the growing communities. Today, chuckwagon cowboys remain independent spirits in a communal enterprise. And their sport, which embodies team sportsmanship, community, and collaboration, is an apt mirror of the Canadian West and a symbol of the character of western Canadians.

In the twenty-first century, chuckwagon cowboys and their sport are an anomaly. Unlike many other professional sports, chuckwagon racing is not dictated by television commercials or primetime viewing audiences. There are no multimillion-dollar contracts. Although they are sports champions, if they do not wear their cowboy hats, the cowboys would need to wear nametags to be recognized — even in Calgary. Chuckwagon cowboys are genuine, commercial free, hell-bent-for-leather westerners, punctuated by rough, wry humour, personal initiative, and gruff compassion.

These men of the prairies are the sport's foundation and its future. In some chuckwagon families, the present drivers are fourth-generation wagon drivers; their great-grandfathers competed with Wildhorse Jack. Preserving family traditions, the cowboys today continue to boast unrivalled personalities.

Buddy Bensmiller, Jim Nevada, and Kelly Sutherland are three such cowboys, whose lives are sweetened by risk. Amidst nickering horses, these cowboys are going to share their triumphs and their trials, their tall tales and their honest-to-God truths, their faults and their dreams.

Both his fans and his peers agree, Buddy Bensmiller is one of the most classy and consistent drivers ever to grip two fistfuls of leather. Born in 1955, the young David Bensmiller was soon called "Buddy" by his family and friends. His acquired name aptly describes this smiling, impressive, unflappable cowboy. Tall, strong, and with a twinkle in his eye, Buddy somehow brings to mind the wide-open spaces roamed by wild horses.

Bensmiller works with horses daily, and he believes he learns more about them every day. Buddy and his wife, Darlene, have four children: Lisa, David, Kurt, and Chance. The family lives on a farm near Dewberry, Alberta. As well as being a supportive father, he is a two-time Calgary Stampede champion and nine-time Cheyenne Frontier Days champion. A former competitor in the Canadian Professional Chuckwagon Association, he now races in the World Professional Chuckwagon Association. Bensmiller is one of the most personable wagon drivers competing, and one of the most accomplished horsemen.

Jim Nevada is a rising chuckwagon superstar. The Nevada family has no previous history in wagon racing, yet Jim continues to stretch his limits — and the sport's. His early struggles to be accepted within chuckwagon racing solidified his devotion to the wagon community and its culture, as well as his zeal to enhance the sport. In 1999, his efforts were acknowledged when he was named the World Professional Chuckwagon Association's Chuckwagon Person of the Year.

Born in 1964, Jim lives outside of Airdrie, Alberta, with his wife, Kim, and their one young son, Will. Nevada is considered one of the finest all-round cowboys in wagon racing and is recognized as perhaps the most dependable outrider of all time. Candid and forthright, he is also filled with dynamic ideas and ambition. Nevada swirls with the invigorating energy of a prairie dust devil.

When people talk about eminent chuckwagon cowboys, they talk about "the King." Kelly Sutherland is to chuckwagon racing what Wayne Gretzky was to hockey, or Michael Jordan was to basketball. Sutherland is the driver to beat.

With his muscular forearms at the ready, Kelly Sutherland carries himself confidently — a chuckwagon gunslinger ready to draw. With assurance, he sports a signature black eagle feather in his cowboy hat. Years ago, young Sutherland gazed at a magnificent bronze chuckwagon trophy and thought, "It'd be satisfying to win one." Thirty years later, he has won nineteen bronze trophies, including eight Calgary Stampede Championships, eight World Championships, and more than sixty other chuckwagon racing championships.

Born in 1951, Kelly Sutherland is indebted to chuckwagons. He often says, "Everything I have, I owe to wagon racing." Kelly and his wife, Debbie, have three children — Tara, Mark, and Mandi — and four grandchildren, and live just outside of Grande Prairie, Alberta. As tough as rawhide, Sutherland is possibly the greatest chuckwagon driver ever, and he remains the sport's fiercest competitor.

Bensmiller, Nevada, and Sutherland are going to show you the view from their driver's seat and give you a personal ride into their emotions and passions. The cowboys' narratives follow their growth into chuckwagon racing — from childhood into parenthood, from rookie into champion. In their subtle Canadian prairie drawls, they tell it like it is: there is no pussy-footin'. And they make no apologies for not bowing to political correctness. They tell their stories in their own words.

What their accounts will show is that chuckwagon cowboys have not received the recognition due them. They remain an uncelebrated brand of western sports star, making ongoing sacrifices on and off the track. Their vocation — of risks and rewards — can be a lonely one. Their stories will strip away the perceived layer of callousness, to reveal sincerity and compassion. Not all of the tears in their eyes are caused by dust.

The lives of Bensmiller, Nevada, and Sutherland exemplify the mythic majesty and transformation of the West. They are imperfect, cuss-chewing heroes amidst expansive prairie landscapes and encroaching suburbia. The cowboys struggle to continue racing behind four swishing tails, while the speeding world chases silent satellites. They have no choice. Proud, they race because that is what they were called to do.

The evening's chuckwagon races are over and the cowboys have finished feeding, watering, and looking after their horses. It is time to wind down and relax. With a chilled can of pop pressed against their bruises, the cowboys are gathering together with their families and friends. You are invited to join this barn party. Please take a seat on a hay bale, and if you'd like some, here's a shot of tonsil varnish. Don't mind the horses; get comfortable. And let's "stretch the blanket."

CHAPTER 1

Seizing the Reins

Seems that I was born to wagon race. Guys would ask my dad, "Should I drive wagons? How do I get started?" His first words always were, "Don't be stupid kid, you don't ever want to start running wagons."

One day, I just looked at him and asked, "Why the hell didn't you tell me that?"

He never said a word.

BUDDY BENSMILLER

Chuckwagon drivers are born with sinewy reins in their hands. They must be, since no chuckwagon curriculum exists, no "Little League Chuckwagons," no entry draft. Even rodeo has riding schools. Chuckwagon cowboys are blessed with a leather-tugging talent, and their abilities are refined through raw experience and the tutelage of fathers, uncles, and friends.

The cowboys' education lies in the wisdom of preceding generations. Wagon-racing preschool often begins with the toddlers sitting next to their fathers in the driver's seat. From this early initiation to horses, the cowboys then usually learn gradually. Jim Nevada describes, "You start as a barn boy, cleaning up the barns, brushing horses, and a little bit of vet work. You wake up, feed horses, walk horses, shovel manure — it's all the grunt work. When you get better with the horses, and if you have any athletic talent, then you start outriding."

While building skills as outriders, the young men may be invited to drive pony chariots and pony chuckwagons. Eventually, if the amateur cowboys continue to demonstrate the compulsory desire, they will be offered the challenge of driving a team of thoroughbreds. Throughout this training, each juvenile driver has a mentor, a veteran to help mould skills, attitudes, and dreams. Sometimes it is a friend, usually it is a family member.

In wagon racing, the number of sons following their fathers into professional competition is a pattern distinctive of the sport. In other professional sports there are situations where sons succeed like their fathers, such as Bobby and Brett Hull in hockey, or the Unser family in auto racing, but they are the rarity rather than the norm. With chuckwagons, it is the opposite. Regularly, the youth are passed the reins from their fathers. The sons learn from their fathers and emulate them. And ultimately, father and son compete together.

From owning their first pony to getting married in a barn, young cowboys are captured by the lure of chuckwagons. To turn their fantasies into reality, the fledgling drivers rely upon the sport's elders for direction. Once they learn the fundamentals, the cowboys must each set their own goals and push their own boundaries. There is no graduation ceremony, but there is acceptance from one's peers, the knowledge of how to rein in self-set priorities, and recognition from one's family.

Kelly Sutherland traces his attraction to wagon racing to an inherited love for horses. Sutherland recalls, "My dad, Max, had an old horse, and I rode him bareback all the time. At five years old, I was too small to jump onto him, so I would go into the pasture and he'd come up to me. I would figure-eight binder twine around his nose, and put a cup of oats on the ground. He'd start eating and I'd jump on his head. When he lifted his head, I slid down onto his back. He'd finish eating, and I'd ride him back to the barn."

At age nine, Sutherland dreamed of becoming a horse veterinarian and began jockeying for his dad. Due to his skinny build, he constantly had runaways on the track. Sutherland reflects, "I never mastered jockeying, and it really frustrated me. People with natural-born talent could outride me, yet I should've been a better rider. I grew up on horses; some of those kids hadn't, but they could sense on a racetrack where they were and how much horsepower they had left." By the time Sutherland was muscular enough to control a thoroughbred, he was too heavy to race. Nevertheless, he adds, "Jockeying quickly taught me what competition was: how much it hurt to lose, and how good it felt to win."

As a lean teenager, Sutherland did win his share of outriding, but he discovered early on that his true gift was racing from behind the horses, rather than on top of them. In the mid-1960s, his father and Dave Lewis, a friend of his father's, had bought a wagon team together. One weekend, when Sutherland was fourteen, he was picking roots with his dad when Lewis called from Wainwright, Alberta, looking for some barn help. Lewis asked, "Max, how about that kid of yours?" Sutherland says, "It was between working as a barn boy or picking roots — not much of a choice."

Kelly Sutherland outrode for two years, and in 1968 he drove at a few autumn shows. In the spring of '69, Lewis asked Kelly if he wanted to drive a wagon full-time. Sutherland recalls, "Ironically, my dad wasn't very happy with Dave letting me drive. I was pretty young, I was only seventeen, kind of scared, and not very strong. I always went hell-bent for leather, but lots of times I was upside down or piled up."

Throughout Sutherland's education, Dave Lewis was his insistent teacher. But Kelly also credits his apprenticeship with Ralph Vigen, who Kelly maintains was the best driver of all time. "Vigen had such a knack about him, but he was a very difficult instructor." He laughs, "He never ever said much. So, I had to watch. I spent hours watching his hands, especially how he turned the barrels. Ralph was by far the best."

In the early 1970s, races and racetracks were designed differently from how they are set up today. Firstly, most races were on short half-mile tracks, compared with the present five-eighth mile. Kelly Sutherland estimates that 50 percent of today's races are won turning barrels, but on the shorter half-mile tracks he puts it at 90 percent. He explains that on the shorter courses, "if the drivers could start and turn [first], they won a ton of races; nobody could pass them. Now with a five-eighth-mile race, a running outfit has more of a chance."

Secondly, all the bottom barrels were positioned high in the infield on sharp right angles to the track. Today, for instance, the bottom barrels of Barrel 4 and Barrel 3 are located on the racetrack itself, allowing the wagons a smooth exit into their lanes, on the track. Previously, when coming around the bottom barrels, the cowboys had to veer their wagons more severely to the left. The horses generated such powerful momentum and twist that the wagons often flipped onto their two right-hand wheels. Each evening of racing, the drivers were threatened with a potential wreck.

Sutherland believes the frequent wrecks did not faze Vigen. "He had zero fear. Usually one wagon upset every night, and sometimes guys got run over — although rarely was anybody hurt badly. While I had butterflies filling my stomach, Ralph had nerves of steel."

Sutherland is indebted to Vigen for tutoring him, not just about racing but also about horsemanship. He says, "Ralph showed me there's no sense trying to beat anything into a wagon horse. You are not going to conquer him with fear." Vigen also taught Kelly how to talk to the horses through the lines. "When I was having trouble driving, he'd get on the wagon seat with me and just grab the lines away. Soon all the horses were galloping along in the right direction. It was really, really strange."

In wagon racing, mentors and fathers are ever hopeful, seeking to motivate their apprentices to master the sport. Kelly Sutherland acknowledges his dad as being the single most important reason for his success. He says, "Dad was always pushing me; for him, there was no second place — none. He was never ever rough physically, but verbally . . . If I screwed up, he told me. He drove it into me. My dad just pushed harder and harder as I started to win."

While Kelly was being bolstered by his father, his mother told him she was so scared she would not watch or attend. Sutherland says, "She never did like the sport because of its inherent danger and risk. She always gave my dad heck that I was driving." He adds, "I'd been hurt as a kid quite a bit. I'd broken my collarbone and my shoulder, and I think she was kind of worried about me." In her early forties, Kelly's mother was diagnosed with multiple sclerosis. Within ten years, she was restricted to a wheelchair, and she continues to fight the disease.

Meanwhile, Sutherland pursued the sport with a fury — his passion to be a champion was unmatched. From his teenage years onward, he was intently focused on winning chuckwagon races. Kelly remembers, "With me it was kind of a sickness, an obsession to win. It just didn't seem like there was anything else. Sometimes when I was a kid, I'd do something wrong and I would cry and think about how stupid it was not to seize an opportunity." He adds, "I always felt the need to prove to somebody who I was, and wagon racing was a vehicle I could do it in. People are born with talents. I soon learned I had a talent driving wagons. I refined it, but not everybody is born with that talent."

Despite his ambitions, Sutherland's premier race in the professional circuit was not an auspicious beginning. After having trained all spring, he hauled his outfit for sixteen hours to his first show ever at Cloverdale, British Columbia, just outside Vancouver. Sutherland reflects, "It was a three-day show, and I never got off the barrels. Each day the horses balked. The horn blew and everything moved but my horses and I. People were laughing. I could have just cried, I was never so embarrassed in all my life." He continues, "The problem was I had a real psycho right-wheeler, an incredible animal. I got him so hot, he just froze. The other horses moved, but they could not move him."

Sutherland went home, and Dave Lewis hooked up a work horse with the right-wheeler. Kelly drove him for a solid week, practising on the barrels. He recalls, "We'd stop in on the barrels, and when we'd holler 'Go!' that work horse would just jerk him ahead so fast outta there." He remembers Lewis saying to him, "That horse will work now. You won't have any more trouble on the barrels." Kelly continues, "Sure enough, I get to Rimbey, Alberta, and when they shot the starter's pistol, I went to the top barrel at a hundred miles an hour. I just cranked the lines and tipped the wagon over. The horses threw me out and took off."

Despite the obvious hazards, Sutherland feels he benefitted by never holding back. He says, "I always went wide open, no matter what. When you are going fast, you learn how to turn barrels and how to drive. You are going to hit a few things and have the odd wreck — that first year I tipped over about three times — but you do learn how to drive."

During his first season, Kelly could be in the top three one day, and in the bottom three the next. He quickly realized that he had to be consistent, to be a champion. Late in that first season, Sutherland won the second-largest show at Morris, Manitoba, and the next year he won at Cheyenne's Frontier Days. His confidence was building, and he was becoming even more aggressive on the track.

His insistence to win at all costs stunned his competitors and fans. He admits, "People couldn't reason I would be so competitive. It took the older guys by surprise. I lived and breathed the sport to win, and to beat the Tom Dorchesters, the Bobby Cosgraves, the Ronnie Glasses. I would do anything to win . . . within the rules. I was driven." He adds, "I remember a '69 headline: 'Wild Man Sutherland.' I had this obsession just to go fast all the time — as fast as I could — but I didn't know where the heck I was going. I was running into wagons, coming wide, tipping over. Definitely in today's sport, I would be disciplined; I would have been sitting on the fence more than I would have been sitting on a wagon seat."

"I practised a lot when I was young," he says, confessing he did so to improve his self-assurance. "At that time, we raced two outfits each night, and we learned to turn barrels, feed lines through our hands, and see how horses reacted after the horn went. We could experiment different ways to turn faster and quicker. I still believe the majority of wagon races are won in the first ten seconds. It is very, very difficult to beat someone coming from behind, and it is important to have the confidence to be out in front."

In the early 1970s, wagon racing did not carry the same profile it does today. Grandstands were smaller, prize money was petty, and there were fewer competitors. Sutherland soon figured out that he only had to defeat the three cowboys who won most of the races. In 1974, at age twenty-two, Sutherland became the youngest victor ever to win the Calgary Stampede.

From the moment he first could straddle a pony, Buddy Bensmiller has adored horses. Bensmiller, along with his four brothers and four sisters, grew up on horseback. "Every day in the spring I rode a different thoroughbred horse to school, just for exercise. I galloped them the entire three and a half miles to Dewberry. If we wanted to go anywhere or visit with the neighbours, it was all done on ponies and saddlehorses." By age seven, he was already jockeying racehorses. "All the picnics had pony races, and we all had a pony." Bensmiller observes, though, that "even though we all grew up with horses, I am the only family member who owns a horse today."

The Bensmiller family was originally from the United States. Buddy Bensmiller's grandfather moved his family to Canada from

Oklahoma around 1900. Although his grandfather was a fine horseman, it was Buddy's father, Allan, who brought chuckwagon racing into the family. Buddy says, "He started in the late forties. My dad didn't win the big shows that I've won, but he went summers that he won every show he entered — fourteen or fifteen shows. Back then, the guys would just get together and race, and the horses Dad raced with were also the horses that he farmed with."

The lanky Buddy Bensmiller began his outriding career when he was twelve. He started outriding at the smaller circuit shows. After only four years, Dallas Dorchester invited Buddy to outride at the Calgary Stampede. Buddy chuckles, remembering his first race, "Before hitting Calgary, I was used to all these little towns. I looked at all those people, and I was so excited I jumped right over the goddam horse. I'm still teased about that."

Bensmiller's mother never saw Buddy ride at Calgary. She had died of cancer the year before, when he was fifteen. At age seventeen, Bensmiller was planning on again outriding at Calgary, but his dad, who was not racing at the Stampede, hoped Buddy would outride for his wagon outfit in the northern Alberta circuit. Buddy told his dad he was going to Calgary unless he was given his own wagon to drive. Bensmiller says, "He did, and that's how I started driving."

Buddy wanted to quit school early. He feels he never had the patience, and says, "I was one of them kids who knew more than the teacher." His father told him, "It's entirely up to you, but you're going to work." So Buddy, despite having no licence, began driving logging trucks in the northern Alberta bush. After his second year of working, Buddy spent his new wealth on horses. Soon, he purchased a freight truck to haul cattle, logs, gravel — anything that could pay for more horses.

The passion Bensmiller and fledgling cowboys throw into the sport springs not only from a craving to win, but also from the sense of family and camaraderie created. Kindred spirits united by the bond of horses, these child cowboys grow up playing together and showing off in front of each other. They share their summers and the most memorable moments in their lives. The cowboys can become like brothers.

Buddy Bensmiller and his friend George Normand were two such young cowboys. Bensmiller met Normand at Meadow Lake, Saskatchewan, when each boy still had to jump up to put his foot into the stirrup. Buddy was jockeying racehorses and George was riding in gymkhana. (At gymkhanas, the horse community — including boys and girls, men and women — competes in such events as barrel racing and various other equestrian games. The competitions test both the riders' and their horses' skill.) Bensmiller says of that first encounter with Normand, "He was just a little French-Canadian, a lot smaller than me . . . and I wasn't very big." From that meeting, they remained best friends, even though Normand lived in Bonnyville, sixty miles away.

Their friendship revolved around their mutual adoration of horses. As teenagers, they drove pony chariots, surviving some jarring and bruise-filled wrecks. Bensmiller describes, "One time, George and I we were racing chariots at Grand Centre [in Alberta] — we were no more than fourteen years old. There was an old guy on the rail, George was in the middle, and I was on the outside. George and that old guy locked wheels. George was thrown out, and landed on his hands and knees between my horses. Amazingly, my horses didn't hit him, but as my chariot ran over him, the axle hit his ass and back. He was scraped up a little, but not hurt very much.

"Normand was 'tough terrible' at chariot racing," Bensmiller recalls. "Another time, his horses got on either side of a rail fence; it stopped his chariot and shot him out like a cannon. He really got beat up that time too. I think he wanted to live a little longer, so he got out of chariots and into wagon racing."

On one afternoon, Normand and Bensmiller decided to hook up some wagon horses while Normand's dad was working. Bensmiller says, "One horse went to kicking and we had a wreck. There was stuff scattered all over the goddam field. We tried to gather it up and get it back into place before his dad got home, but his dad noticed and we got shit . . . a lot of hell, over that."

Bensmiller also pitched in to help Normand drive his outfit when needed. The year Normand started driving, he had a runaway the first night of the show at North Battleford, Saskatchewan. While Normand gamely hung on to the lines, his outfit made another two laps around. An outrider rode up to grab a wheel horse, but in doing so his horse got caught in a wheel and was knocked down. Normand's wagon ran over the horse and the outrider, breaking the outrider's leg. The horse was not seriously harmed. The wreck unnerved Normand, and the next evening Bensmiller graciously drove for him.

Until Normand's death in a chuckwagon accident in 1994, the two men continued to be best friends, sharing horses, practical jokes, and ideas, even when they decided to compete in different chuckwagon circuits — Bensmiller in the CPCA, Normand in the WPCA. They were chuckwagon brothers, including in family life: they stood up for each other at their respective weddings. (Bensmiller was so committed to wagon racing that he and his new wife, Darlene, daughter of wagon driver Allen Smith, shared their honeymoon at a Lloydminster charity wagon race.)

Bensmiller's proficiency in handling horses was inspired and passed down by his father. Horses became their mutual touchstone. Bensmiller says, "As far as I'm concerned there were only two guys who could drive wagons: Dad and Ralph Vigen. No matter what horses they took, they could drive them. My dad, he was a teamster. All his life he drove horses — in the fields, on the track — he never could get away from it."

Bensmiller reflects, "Dad definitely told me when I did something wrong, but he never told me when I did anything right — it didn't hurt me anyway. I've tried to drive like my dad, handling the horses so smoothly. When he was holding the lines, you'd never see a horse fling its head into the air. He had such a great feel for a horse, even with horses other people couldn't drive." He adds, "Dad taught me to be a sportsman. You could not get a more honest man. Attitude will take you a long way in this sport, not only on the racetrack but also with sponsorship."

Bensmiller's driving skills matured, and he has remained indebted to his father's guidance and instruction. Buddy says, "Dad figured it was great I was into wagons. The last few years he was alive, we did a lot together. Even while he was fighting cancer, I'd go harness his team so he could still drive. The harness was too heavy for him then, but he still wanted to sit and drive the horses. He raced till he was sixty-nine years old, when I gave him an outfit to drive at Dewberry for the last time. There are very few people left in this world like my dad, who are horsemen right to the very end."

In contrast to Sutherland and Bensmiller, Jim Nevada did not grow up around horses, nor wagons. Nevada explains, "My grandfather did not like horses, he liked cows." He adds, "I was eleven years old when we moved the twenty kilometres from Airdrie into Calgary. Dad and Mom divorced, and Dad wasn't around any more. I didn't have much of a family back then."

For Nevada, the chuckwagon community became his adopted family, and it nurtured his interest in horses. Just outside of Airdrie lived Nevada's maternal grandparents, and a mile south of their farm lived Ron and Barb David. Ron and his brothers were active chuckwagon drivers, and Nevada began working for Ron as a barn boy. Nevada says, "For two years, between working at my grandparents' farm or at the Davids', I was out in Airdrie every weekend. It was good to be out there, keeping me out of trouble in the city. The Davids' became my second home."

He adds, "At the Davids', I worked to buy my first two horses. The first horse I bought was a quarter horse–Morgan cross, and at age thirteen, that horse was my only transportation. Until I got my driver's licence, we'd be ripping horses back and forth to my friend's place, even when it was forty below." However, the horses were used not just for transportation. Nevada laughs, "We did stupid stuff like horseback 'chicken fights,' or we pulled toboggans, galloping down the ditch, hitting approaches, and seeing how far we could fly. I don't know why we weren't killed, because we did some stupid things. I got quite a few stitches, but was never badly hurt."

Strangely, Nevada first heard a wagon race before he ever saw one. Working for Ron David, he was in the barns and behind the fences at his first race. He remembers, "It was so weird. I heard the wagons running, it was noisier than hell, and I thought, 'Geez, that thing's going to blow apart.'

Nevada, like most drivers, progressed from barn boy to outrider. Generally, the teenaged wagon prodigies are invited to outride when they have the requisite physical strength and agility. From a spectator's viewpoint, outriding seems straightforward: the men throw the items in the wagon, hop on a horse, and follow the wagon. It is not so simple. Nevada explains, "People wonder how hard it is to be an outrider — to run up, jump up on a horse, turn them, and run around the racetrack. Well, certain people are horse people, and certain ones ain't, even if they have been around horses all their life. You've got to have a feel for what the horse is doing. One out of ten guys make it, and that does not guarantee they are any good. There are a lot of barn boys who are too fat, too short, and they cannot jump on a running horse."

Chuckwagon drivers are usually reluctant to hire rookie outriders. The drivers count on the outriders not to make mistakes; their mortgage payments and livelihood may be relying upon the outriders' expertise. They cannot afford a blunder.

Jim Nevada faced these hurdles when he began outriding. "When I first started, Ronnie David hired me, and then he fired me. I was too small to throw the stove in, and I was not good enough to hold the leaders. But I kept at it." By persevering, Nevada quickly developed his natural talents, and drivers began to seek him out and hire him for his reliability. "The first year," he notes, "I would have finished second in the outrider standings, but I was underage and Mom would not sign my membership card. I just went and raced anyway. I got a hundred-dollar fine at the end of the year, but I put seven thousand dollars in the bank. At age fifteen, I was a pretty rich kid."

Outriding tests cowboys. It examines them to see if they have the fortitude, the guts, to compete in this rough-and-tumble sport. And it is the veteran cowboys who are the interrogators. Jim gives an example: "One time, at Morris, Manitoba, I was riding for

Ronnie, and two outriders tried to box me in. If I was late, Ronnie lost the show; if I was on time, he won it. Another older outrider, who used a piece of garden hose for a riding crop, went riding through, and instead of hitting his horse he was hitting those two. He opened up the way for me." He adds, "After the race, he told those two, 'If you want to carry this on, we can go back to the barns.' They were tough enough to do it on the track, but they were not man enough to fight behind the barns."

Unlike the fathers of other chuckwagon cowboys, Nevada's father had nothing to do with wagons, nor with his son. Jim was ten years old when his father left home, disappearing from his life, and Jim did not see him again until fourteen years later. He describes the scene, "I was twenty-four, and I was outriding at the Calgary Stampede, sitting on a horse, ready to go out for a race, when I heard, 'Hey, son!' I looked up, and here is a guy who'd put on a little weight and lost a little hair. I didn't recognize him. It didn't click. So I looked back down where I was going to ride, and I hear, 'Yeah you, son!' There was the old man."

Nevada states, "My dad had no time for me, and the only time he did was when I had done something, and made something of myself. My dad had no involvement. He died in '97 of lung cancer, during the Calgary Stampede."

His mother, meanwhile, initially tried everything to stop him from racing, and Jim did everything he could to pursue it. He says, "Chuckwagon racing really is not known as a safe sport. If Mom had her way, I would not be doing it, but now she is probably my loudest fan in the whole grandstand — she is very vocal."

After experiencing success as an outrider, Nevada, with the help of Ron David, purchased some thoroughbreds and started driving. His first solo practice in the driver's seat was far from promising. He recounts, "Ronnie helped hook up the horses, and said, 'Okay, you're on your own.' But my friend Crazy Harold jumped into the wagon. We took off down a cultivated field, and a bridle was falling off a wheel horse. We're going faster and faster — finally we're going full tilt. I yelled to Harold to grab the wheeler's lines, to keep the bit in. Harold jumps out.

"At that speed, when Harold's feet hit the ground, his head was driven into the dirt. Finally, I just kept turning the leaders into a jackknifed stop, with the wagon tilted up on an angle. Ronnie pulls up in his truck, and he's laughing so hard, he falls to the ground on his knees. He couldn't help us get untangled or going again, he was laughing so hard."

Whether his mentors were lecturing him or deriving amusement at his expense, Nevada relied upon them for guidance. Both Ronnie David and Richard Cosgrave were instrumental in his training. He says, "At the races, Richard would haul me aside and give me shit. Richard told me, 'Any asshole can take the four horses out there, turn the barrels, run around the racetrack once, and call themselves a wagon driver. That's not a wagon driver, Jim. Learn to drive a horse. Take the four horses, hook 'em up, and drive them. Drive around the field, stop, hold the horses, have a smoke. Get to know your horses.'"

Nevada admits, "When I first started driving, I'd hook the horses, blast them through the barrels, run them in the field till there was foam coming out of their mouths, take them to the barn, let them walk out and drink up — and I called myself a wagon driver. Now, in the spring, I work them in the corral, then with a harness, then I hook two horses, then four, and I do not run them till a week before the first show. I get them in condition, in shape, and muscled up."

Kelly moves in front down the backstretch at High River, Alberta, June 15, 1996.
(CAROL AND PAUL EASTON, WAGON PHOTOGRAPHY)

Kelly makes a move on the outside at Hayworth Stables, outside of Strathmore, Alberta, June 6, 1998. (CAROL AND PAUL EASTON, WAGON PHOTOGRAPHY)

Wearing his signature black eagle feather, Kelly keeps the lead in the backstretch at High River, Alberta, June 15, 1997. (CAROL AND PAUL EASTON, WAGON PHOTOGRAPHY)

Kelly turns the top barrel with his left leader, "Ralph," at Strathmore, Alberta, July 31, 1998. (CAROL AND PAUL EASTON, WAGON PHOTOGRAPHY)

Kelly gives his "thumbs up," with $50,000 cheque in hand, on stage at the Calgary Stampede in 1998. (SUTHERLAND FAMILY COLLECTION)

FOLLOWING SPREAD: Kelly snaps the lines, urging his horses to the finish at High River, Alberta, June 12, 1998. (CAROL AND PAUL EASTON, WAGON PHOTOGRAPHY)

Kelly holds the bronze trophy from his first Calgary Stampede Rangeland Derby victory, in 1974. (SUTHERLAND FAMILY COLLECTION)

Nevada remains grateful for Cosgrave's help. Other drivers did not seem willing to give him the tips he needed, even when he asked. He feels Cosgrave was one of the few drivers who cared, and the one who gave him the reassuring pat on the back he needed.

Nevada believes drivers who come from a wagon-racing family enjoy support he never had, both emotionally and financially. He says, "Guys like Buddy had their fathers to talk to. I never had that help or luxury. I couldn't go to Dad and ask, 'Can I borrow your right-hand leader?' It's like borrowing the family car. The odd time, I'd make a deal where I would outride for a driver and he'd loan me his left-hand leader. Ninety-nine percent of the time the horse they lent me was not a left-hand leader but a horse that held a freakin' collar around its neck."

Because he lacked the family assistance and resources, it took Jim longer to become competitive. He says, "The first eight years I was borrowing junk and buying other guys' junk." He could only afford other drivers' second-rate horses, or else he borrowed older horses from Ron David. But for inexperienced drivers, racing veteran horses poses problems. "The older, smarter horses are tougher to drive than younger ones," says Nevada. "The new ones don't know where they are going, so they will go wherever you point them, but the older ones are like pushing a piece of string. They duck, dive, and they know how to get out of working; they know where they are going before you do. Those are the horses I drove the first few years, and holy, it was quite a learning experience."

Looking back, Nevada considers, "It wasn't pretty, some of the crap I hooked, but I think it made me a better driver, because when I got to the good horses, I could really drive them."

The young cowboys' eagerness for wagon racing was fashioned into real skill by the veterans. Whittled, nurtured, and refined, the novices' driving abilities blossomed. Their apprenticeship was complete. Now they would determine their own success, deciding for themselves what the sport meant to them. They would have to prove whether they had the enduring spirit, pluck, and enterprise of chuckwagon racing's pioneers.

Horses, competition, and family and friends — these are the components that have harnessed Sutherland, Bensmiller, and Nevada to the sport. These factors compelled the young men to place the gifts of their youth under the wagon canvas. And they remain the foundations of the chuckwagon lifestyle, spurring on these cowboys to realize their childhood dreams.

CHAPTER 2

Chasing the Gold Buckle Dream

I find in other things I do, I'm obsessed by having to win. I am always in a hurry or a race. It is probably not a healthy attitude to have, except in wagon racing. Even now, when Debbie and I sit down to have dinner, I'll be done, waiting, and she'll say, "Well, you won that race." Maybe I should take some time to savour the food.

KELLY SUTHERLAND

From June to August, the cowboys and the chuckwagon cavalcade roam the prairies. Moving from show to show, they haul their horses and their families. They pursue the shiny buckles awaiting each show's champion. Going after their ambitions, the cowboys gallivant from northern British

Columbia to sometimes as far down as southern California. It is an arduous schedule punctuated with laughter and rivalry, and the constant support of the wagon community.

The chuckwagon community is an extended family. This is visibly demonstrated when a retired driver dies: members of the community will drive from across the prairies, even in the heart of winter, to ensure they attend the funeral. When you become part of the chuckwagon clan, membership lasts a lifetime. And membership is well earned. Chronic injuries, endless chores, and personal bankruptcy are all costs incurred in pursuing wagons. Even marriages have been lost to wagons, as wives may discover they will always play second-fiddle to horses.

However, cowboys acknowledge the importance of the support they receive from their wives and girlfriends. Wagon women are counsellors, lovers, and bolsterers. They join in with doing the chores, mending the horses, or cleaning the mud-soaked harnesses. Women and children are also relied upon at the racetrack, helping to exercise and cool down the horses. Wagon racing is a family enterprise. And it is this simple fact that accounts for the ongoing allure of the sport. Jim Nevada sums it up: "The people and a love of horses are the main reasons why people race. It's one big family. If you lost the people or horses, you might as well quit."

Kelly Sutherland had his own family before he finished high school. Kelly met his future wife, Debbie, in high school — he was fifteen and she was fourteen. In a year, Debbie was pregnant. She was sent to Edmonton to have the baby and was instructed to give the child up. Sutherland says, "Debbie phoned me when Tara was born and said she was bringing her home. Debbie stayed with her mom for a couple of months, but it was not easy for her, since her mom and dad had split up. Debbie told me, 'Let's get married,' and I said, 'What the hell.' So at seventeen, I quit school and went to work in the oil field up north."

Sutherland continues, "I think in the first six years of marriage, if there had been anywhere for her to go, she probably would have left. She was scared of horses, but she soon learned if we were going to stay married she'd have to come with me. When you're eighteen, there's a lot of hormonal urges going on, and a lot of young girls running around after cowboys. Her mom and dad had moved away, so Debbie decided to join me on the road." Reflecting on that period, he adds, "We had grown up together, but basically had not learned to live with each other."

Sutherland feels his relationship with Debbie has definitely contributed to his ability to win. He says, "You need that mental support behind you. Any champion has got to be told he's a champion. It makes him a step above other people, and into an arrogant type of individual who has so much self-confidence that he can achieve what he believes he can achieve. He's got to be dressed up and down, and usually that comes from behind the scenes. I firmly believe that — in any sport."

Jim Nevada also met his future wife in high school. "I was a teacher's assistant for phys. ed. class, and I taught Kim scuba diving. She knew what a wagon race was, but she'd never seen one. I told her I was an outrider, and she said, 'Yeah, right.' I was captain of the football team, and she thought I was just a jock." He also remembers, "At school, even though I was a cowboy and had some buckles, I still wore running shoes and Levi's. A lot of the kids around the school wanted to be cowboys. They had a cowboy hat, cowboy boots, and a Kmart buckle . . . I never even owned a cowboy hat."

For Jim and Kim, it was a typical chuckwagon high school romance. They were together throughout the school year, but broke up in the summertime when he was going down the road, outriding all wagon season. Nevada says, "I was never home during the summer, so it didn't make much sense to have a girlfriend."

Nevada adds, "Kim was attracted to a cowboy even though she is allergic to horses and dust. Not only that, but Kim is actually too nice to be around chuckwagon people. She was ten by the time she had heard all the swear words I had heard by age three. She grew up in Calgary at a Catholic school, moved to small-town Airdrie, and her first locker partner was pregnant.

"But it must have been meant to be. Kim and I have been together ever since."

Restricted by her allergies, Kim Nevada nevertheless contributes to the chuckwagon lifestyle, but in ways that do not entail horses. Jim says, "She fits in with the chuckwagon people, but she doesn't fit in with the work and that's mainly because of her allergies to dust. There are just some people who are good around horses, and she's not; she's scared of horses. But she's happy, and helps out by making us food to eat. It doesn't bug me at all. I like it the way it is." He adds, "I see some wives who are quite involved, and I don't think I could handle that. Some of the women never shut up. I don't know how some of the guys put up with it. There is just a lot to figure out about the horses all summer."

Women who become seduced by the sport, or by a wagon cowboy, understand it is a male-dominated sport. In pro chuckwagon racing, no woman has yet competed as a driver. Controlling the horses during the races demands considerable physical strength. Kelly Sutherland says, "If a woman did have a great attraction to wagon racing, she usually married a chuckwagon driver, or took the guy she married and made him into one."

Although they are restricted from driving, over the decades, there have been a few female outriders. Sutherland feels more women might compete if outriding meant only jockeying, but he suggests, "They've got to be more 'western.' It's kind of rough." Just like the West, the sport is wild, furious, and unrestrained. From his outrider's experience, Jim Nevada believes wagon women do have their opinions on how outriders should perform. He comments, "One thing you learn is every wagon wife is an expert on outriders. They've ridden a thousand heats, they're all experts, and you never argue with them."

Buddy Bensmiller's wife, Darlene, is involved with the doctoring and treating of injured or ailing horses. Remarkably, says Buddy, "Darlene and I rarely talk about wagon racing." Darlene adds, "I never tell him what to hook or what to do, that's his department. If he doesn't know by now, he sure doesn't need me telling him."

During the summer wagon season, Bensmiller wants his family with him on the road. He says, "Darlene still travels with me, but the kids are old enough to stay in school now. They used to travel with us when they were younger. It wouldn't be worth it if they couldn't be there. Lots of guys like to drive away and leave the family behind, but I never was that way. If it's not a family commitment, you're not going to give it one hundred percent."

Bensmiller also recognizes that his family relies upon his talents. He shares, "Everybody says I do it for the money, but the money's payin' for very few of us. There's no doubt about it — if

I wasn't making money, I wouldn't be doing it. A guy's got a family to raise, and you've got to think of them. There are so many guys out there not making a nickel, and as far as I'm concerned, the family is hurting from it."

Buddy emphasizes, "There are guys, no matter what horses they had, they don't have the ability or the 'want' to make it happen. It's a big commitment. To be a chuckwagon driver is no big deal, but to shoot for a World championship or a Calgary Stampede championship, it takes a lot of hard work. A lot of other parts of your life hurt because of what you've got to do with these horses. It's just a damn good thing my family enjoys it, 'cause how do you put the hours in if they're unhappy? They all understand basically what I want, and that makes it a lot easier. I didn't miss too many birthday parties, but I will miss their wedding if they have it during the summertime."

Not only does Bensmiller's family respect his ambitions, but so do friends and the community of Dewberry. To enable Buddy and Darlene to attend important events, a number of friends have gone as far as to reschedule wedding dates, and the local school has even changed their children's graduation dates. The whole town offers support to Bensmiller.

The people of Dewberry respect the dedication Buddy brings to wagons and his horses. All year long, they expect to see him out with his horses. Bensmiller remarks, "The neighbours are good. In the spring, when we're breaking horses and the fields are too soggy, our neighbours watch out for us as we drive our teams down the side of the road."

And Dewberry is unabashedly proud of its local chuckwagon racers, including Bruce Craige, who won the Calgary Stampede in 1981. The community is home to "the world's largest racing chuckwagon." The chuckwagon, twice the size of a normal wagon, is pulled by draught horses in parades and otherwise rests prominently throughout the year in an open shelter at the high end of the town's main street. Also, the local museum exhibits photographs of Buddy's father and his horses, as well as some of his father's wagon trophies.

Across the West, chuckwagon racing is intertwined with community and family. From wooing a date from the wagon seat, to making love in the wagon box, to perhaps dying under a wagon's wheels: such events are part and parcel of the lives of the people who are bound to chuckwagons. All the drivers agree that the wagon community is an extension of their own family. It is this kinship that sets wagon racing apart from most sports. Bensmiller says, "There's nothing that compares with the relationships. If a guy does have a little bad luck, everyone jumps in to help. You don't find that in a lot of other sports."

Kelly Sutherland describes the wagon tribe, "For the most part they are rural based people and animal lovers. They are also family oriented people. In a thirty-year career, we spend four to five months together, living like gypsies, in some cases literally inches or feet apart. Naturally you're going to get close with some people, you're going to fight with some people too, but they're all part of the community. Some of those people, you get to know them better than your own brothers. You spend more time with them. There's quite a bond there all the time, and there's not a lot of people who come in and out." Kelly adds, "Unlike rodeo, we're closer. Rodeo competitors only compete once at an event by themselves. We move like a big family; for five days we move, sit for a week, and then move again." However, Buddy Bensmiller concedes, "There is the odd little spat, but you expect that. Even families have them."

The seasonal migration of chuckwagon life is normal for these men and women. Bensmiller began living in trailers and trucks when he was seven years old. He says, "We used to sleep under trucks. When it rained, we put hay bales underneath the truck, to get up and off the wet ground." Nowadays, Bensmiller's sponsor loans him a sparkling new recreational vehicle each summer. The rest of the wagon community also travels in recreational vehicles and well-used motorhomes.

Wagon people were even more vital to Jim Nevada's upbringing. Even though Nevada at times struggled to be accepted and supported by the wagon community, he says, "For most, it is their second family; and for me, the way I grew up, it was my number one family. Just like any family, you've got your cousins that you like, and the cousins that are inbred and you hate. But we aren't just a bunch of hicks. Most of the sponsors can't believe what a close-knit group it is. If I get hurt, there are ten people there to help me out."

The community rallies together to offer assistance when a member is injured. For example, driver Orville Strandquist's son incurred a disabling injury, and although it did not result from a wagon race, the wagon community raised the money to purchase a modified van. Auctions are held to raise money for wounded outriders, and a benevolent fund — supported by outriders' donations — is designated for injured outriders.

Competing as outriders and drivers are many Native cowboys. They are an integral part of the chuckwagon community. The sport brings Native and non-Native people together, uniting them in their common passion to race horses. Ribbing is common among the cowboys; the humour can be bawdy, but it is good natured. Jim

Nevada grins, "There are a lot of Indians in the sport, but like they told me, they've been chasing wagons for hundreds of years." The exceptional horsemanship skills of Native cowboys have propelled them to wagon-racing distinction. For example, Edgar Baptiste, who hails from the Red Pheasant reservation, near Cando, Saskatchewan, outran Kelly Sutherland, Dallas Dorchester, and Tyler Helmig to win the Calgary Stampede in 1996.

When the wagon trucks arrive at a show, the golf clubs come out with the feed buckets. Many cowboys are as handy with a nine iron as they are with four lines. Jim Nevada says, "Chuckwagons are perfect for golfing because we always race at night. So during the afternoon we can play nine holes; and if you get someone to feed oats at noon, you can play eighteen holes. One year I golfed over forty times. When we were younger we went to the swimming holes; now we go golfing."

Even on the links, the cowboys cannot escape their craving to race. Nevada explains, "If you jam a golf tee into a golf cart's governor, you can get an extra twenty miles per hour. One time, driver Doyle Mullaney was about to take a shot; I roared past him, hit the brakes, and did three complete spins right in front of him. I just laughed."

The cowboys' contests have also carried on after the evening's races. In Regina, Saskatchewan, Nevada and friends once participated in the first documented game of "Full Contact Beer Gardens Football." Nevada remembers, "A chuckwagon appreciation dinner was hosted inside an arena, and locals challenged us to a football game. Guys were running down the middle of tables, between people sitting enjoying a beer. The arena cleared out pretty quickly." He continues, "More time was spent running across the tables than running on the sand floor. Guys jumped over one table, hit a guy on another table, and flew onto a different table. There was no equipment, and many stitches. It was so rough it only lasted one game."

Jim Nevada says these capers were typical during his rowdy days outriding. For fifteen years, Nevada used to race and then head to the beer garden. Today, the sport and its athletes are more professional. "Outriders must be responsible, or the drivers won't hire you," emphasizes Nevada. "If people realize you're out partying all night instead of getting your sleep, you won't last too long."

Jim also suggests that the cowboys now throw more bowling balls than beer bottles. "In High River we've gone bowling, and it's funnier than heck to see thirty wagon drivers in the bowling alley. Instead of beer gardens and bars, its golf courses and bowling alleys." He adds, "Everybody's grown up a bit, and they can still have fun without partying all night. Now the best times are staying back in the barns and having a few drinks. Somebody pulls out a guitar, and we chirp and sing. People see a campfire, and they come to sit around and have a big bullshit session. It is a lot of fun, and the sponsors like it too."

Within the barns, friendly bets and dares are commonplace. Nevada describes one such running bet: "Dennis Janice had oat-eating contests with a horse. He would wager he could eat a gallon of oats faster than a horse. We'd have a few beers, put a gallon oats in front of Dennis, a gallon in front of the horse, put the money on the table, and the race was on."

Nevada asserts, "Sometimes he beat the horse."

Buddy Bensmiller remarks, "That's one thing about wagon racing — there's always a good laugh."

In chasing the circuit, the wagon drivers face high transportation costs. The cowboys have to invest thousands of dollars to maintain their stable of vehicles: trucks, horse liners, trailers, and recreational vehicles. They haul their horses, chuckwagons, and families up to 5,000 miles each summer. To finance their summer racing, emerging wagon drivers must take on extra work throughout the winter.

As a young driver, Kelly Sutherland says he "lived and breathed horses." To cover his costs, Kelly lived in a truck for six months every winter, working in the northern Alberta oil patch, while Debbie raised their young family. When March arrived, the next six months revolved around training, racing, and maintaining horses.

Buddy Bensmiller echoes the driver's commitment: "I worked hard all winter, just to race in the summertime." Bensmiller trucked for over twelve years. In his first winter trucking, he and George Normand worked for forty-five days in the bush to earn the money to buy horses. Buddy says, "Horses were all we talked about — how many and which ones we would buy."

During spring training, Bensmiller would wake up at 5 a.m., drive a truck all day, and return home at 9 p.m. As dusk fell, he would then haul his horses three miles to the Dewberry racetrack to practise. By the time they were finished and the horses unhooked, it was dark. The next morning, Bensmiller was back at work.

Bensmiller suggests, "Today's young guys won't do that. If they have to work the next day, they'll feed the horses, but they won't hook them." However, he admits there may not be too many cowboys who would have done it then. He says, "You've got to 'love' it; I guess that's the word for it. A lot of people kind of figure

I'm crazy. They drive by and it's thirty below, and I'm out there with a work team, but it makes no difference to me."

To support his wagon ambitions, Jim Nevada worked varying winter jobs, including driving freight trucks and selling insurance. He admits he started off with nothing, and is indebted to his friends and family for enabling him to go down the road. He says, "Sure, I had to work two jobs, but my friends and my grandparents helped a lot."

In the early 1990s, however, Nevada's attempts to establish his career as a driver with his own outfit had stalled, and his wife, Kim, suggested that he quit. Her comments touched a raw nerve. Jim explains, "I've never been a quitter, no matter what I did. If I start something, I'm going to finish it; but it was taking me longer than probably anyone else to succeed in the sport. I couldn't afford it." He recalls, "She kept saying to me, 'You're a helluva outrider. Why don't you keep outriding horses and rent them out to make money?' We were living in an apartment and all of our money was going towards the horses, with little results. I had to do a lot of outriding to pay the bills, and that affected my outfit, since I wasn't spending enough time with the horses. I didn't want to be an outrider all my life, yet here's someone I'm married to telling me different."

Nevada was struggling to such an extent that he was planning on quitting. That's when his corporate sponsor, Trail Appliances, through Paul Broderick and Gail Giroux, came to Nevada's rescue. They restored his confidence by telling him, "Here's fifteen thousand dollars, Jim. Go buy yourself some decent horses." Nevada found some quality horses, requalified for Calgary, and began to win again. "If it wasn't for Trail, I'd probably be done racing or divorced," he states.

"Kim was making suggestions that I should do something else," says Nevada, "and it was at a point in my life when I started to think about our future. Looking back, I agree, there were grounds for complaining. If it had come to either her or chuckwagons, I probably would've picked chuckwagons. It was getting that bad. I'm glad it never got that way, but if I hadn't made the Calgary Stampede, it may well have gone that way."

Having qualified for Calgary, and benefitting from the influx of expanded sponsorship dollars, Jim was able to reinvest in his cattle-raising and wagon operations. This positive turnaround offered both Kim and Jim some hope. Jim realized he needed some land. And since his grandparents had told him they were planning to stay on the family farm, Jim bought his own property. He says, "Grandpa and I are two pigheaded people and we went nose to nose on lots of arguments. When he saw me buy other land, he realized I was committed. He saw something in me, and offered me the family farm. Their generosity helped out a lot, and everything started going in the right direction."

He beams, "Now Kim's glad I stuck with it."

As an unknown driver with no family member preceding him into the sport — and hence no "wagon family name" — Jim Nevada understands the need to create and successfully market a personal image. He took advantage of the associations people would make with his surname, "Nevada." On his saddle blankets, and on each side of his wagon box, are a pair of dice. The apt logo also underscores the crapshoot gamble of wagon racing.

Jim Nevada's trademark "coontail" was also designed for visibility. He describes, "When I outrode, Mom nagged that she couldn't pick me out during a race. She had given me a racoon tail key chain, so I taped the coontail to the back of my outriding helmet. With the coontail, I won Calgary four times."

For fourteen years, Nevada's coontail bounced around the racetrack. He adds, "It was the only one, but one year at Calgary, six riders from the other wagon association were wearing coontails. That really pissed me off. It was a Davy Crockett convention. I just walked up to those guys and said, 'Can't you think up anything on your own?' When they saw how mad I was, three guys got rid of them, but not all of them. I ripped my tail off my helmet, threw it in a mud puddle, and walked away. We each have our own coat of arms, and mine was the coontail. It's a sore spot that others still use it."

Meanwhile, Kelly Sutherland was labelled with the illustrious title of "the King." He attributes this regal brand to announcer Joe Carbury — "the Voice of the Calgary Stampede." Sutherland explains, "Canadian Rodeo News ran a headline entitled 'The King of Chuckwagon Racing,' but Joe Carbury is the individual who used it during the races. Carbury would announce, 'Here comes the King and all the King's men.'"

Sutherland admits, "No doubt, I've probably won more than anyone else, but they used 'the King' long before I had won so much. It may have been because of the type of individual I was — a pusher, a leader, trying to lead the organization."

Sutherland is also well known for giving a vigorous "thumbs up" as he completes the post-race parade past the grandstand. He grins, "That started years ago. Every time I go into a race, I want to stick it in the ass of my competitors so far [that] they never know what happened. I don't hate those drivers, but I have always been driven. I'll just do anything to beat those individuals. When

I'm finished, and if I have had a really good race, I'm just so elated. Somehow, I've just got to show the public those emotions, and that's where the thumbs up originated."

But Kelly Sutherland's most identifiable trademark is the eagle feather attached to his black cowboy hat. He connects himself with the Native cultures' spiritual respect for eagle feathers. He states, "In 1974, in Ponoka, Alberta, I started wearing a feather. I was having a run of bad luck, and I told my buddy Mark Wagner, 'This is the worst summer I have ever had. I don't know what it is; no matter what I do something goes wrong.'" Kelly says that Wagner told him, "Your luck must be the shits. You take this eagle feather, tie it into your hat, and see what happens." Sutherland continues, "I'm not overly superstitious, but that's the first year I won Calgary. For quite a while, I didn't want to change anything, and it became a tradition."

Buddy Bensmiller's label is found on the side of his wagon. His friend George Normand always raced with chrome steer heads screwed to either side of his wagon box. The steer heads were George's good luck charms. Following the wagon accident in 1994, in which Normand was killed, Bensmiller removed the steer heads, straightened them out, and reattached them to his own wagon. This gleaming western image is a reminder of the brotherhood forged in wagon racing, and the responsibility to friendship.

As for his marketing emphasis, Bensmiller places it on entertaining people. He says, "I like to put on a show for the crowd. If I go out and screw up, then I feel bad because I didn't put on a good enough show for the people who came through the gate. If you get beat by a nose, fine; if you get beat by three lengths, that's bad. It's tough to do it day after day, and some drivers realize that more than others. The only pressure I have is screwing up in front of a crowd.

"I don't care where the people come from — across the water, through the bushes — if you ask them what really rattled their chains at the Calgary Stampede, the first thing they will say is the wagons. That's the way it should be." Bensmiller adds, "I get letters from kids, men, women, who appreciate the sport so much for what a guy does for it, or does in it. That means a lot to me."

Not every fan appreciates the cowboys with the same clarity. "Some outsiders think we are a little different to do this sport," Bensmiller laughs. "In the States, people often came up to me and said, 'Geez, you *are* human.'"

Beginning in the 1930s, Cheyenne's Frontier Days hosted one of the most challenging shows on the wagon circuit. The show featured mainly Canadian drivers, who were billed as "The Wildest Wheels in Wyoming" and "The Thunder from the North." Buddy Bensmiller won the coveted Cheyenne buckle nine times, but it was not simply the buckles taking him south of the border. "The Americans go crazy," he explains. "They really like wagon racing. That's why I always liked Cheyenne, because I've never been to a place anywhere where the people get so into it. When you came out of the barrels, the whole crowd just came alive. After winning a race, there were twelve thousand people standing and screaming. It's hard to explain. You just don't get that in Canada." Buddy adds, "I have always enjoyed running wagons. I didn't care where, but I stayed with the CPCA so I could race at Cheyenne."

Bensmiller also took satisfaction in chatting to American visitors about chuckwagons. "In Wyoming," he says, "my barn was always where the people walked by. I could talk about wagons all day." A personable ambassador for the sport, Bensmiller opened many eyes — including those of singer Garth Brooks — to the demands of operating a wagon outfit. Presently, the professional wagons are not running in Cheyenne, but Bensmiller's positive impact on the American perception of wagon cowboys endures.

Away from the barns and on the street, chuckwagon drivers are harder to pin down. Jim Nevada explains, "There is a difference between the chuckwagon driver and the rodeo cowboy. Most of us wear baseball caps, running shoes, a belt and buckle, and we're horsemen. I consider myself a cowboy and a horseman, but more of a horseman. There are a few who wear cowboy hats all the time, but I only wear one when I am representing wagons." He adds, "When you wear a damn cowboy hat, ninety percent of the time it gets wrecked flying off in a wagon race anyway. Dirty horses run over it, and you have to reshape it every second day. So I've got a good hat, and a hat I wear racing."

For Nevada, the cowboy image is not as meaningful as the cowboy within. "I see guys with three-hundred-dollar ostrich boots and a thousand-dollar buckle," he says, "and they couldn't ride a stick horse. I kind of laugh at that. I don't push that I'm a cowboy, but I'm proud of being a cowboy." Nevada also feels rodeo cowboys get more recognition and are more revered than wagon cowboys. "Cowboys, like bull rider Tuff Hedeman, are heroes all year, whereas we're heroes two months of the year, and especially ten days at Calgary. Other than that, no one really cares who we are." He adds, "I don't think wagon racing's the kind of sport cowboys should have an ego about, cause it's not that great of a sport. It's not like NHL hockey, where you can walk down the street and be recognized."

Unlike Nevada, Bensmiller and Sutherland both do wear a cowboy hat regularly. It is part of their identity, and it is their means of promoting themselves and the sport. Bensmiller worries about other drivers' seeming lack of appreciation for the sport's western image. He says, "I go around the barns and see young drivers with ball caps on backwards and shorts on. There's no cowboy hat, there are no cowboy boots — instead there are running shoes and sweat pants. It's a thrill for the sponsors to get to the barns; but if the guys are in their sweat pants, it doesn't look the same to me." Bensmiller is concerned that the sponsors who support wagon racing's western identity are not receiving their money's worth. He laments, "What is this for the sponsor and the public to see? The West has gone out of it. Where the hell is it going?"

In wagon racing, sponsorship translates into companies, or pooled groups of individuals, purchasing the rights to advertise on the wagon tarps. The sponsors are integral benefactors of the sport. Through partnerships that can last for years, the sponsors often become part of the drivers' extended families. Sometimes, the sponsors become more competitive than the drivers, hungry to defeat their business rivals on the track.

Initially, the Calgary Stampede allowed only the names of individuals to appear on wagon tarps, so naturally all the drivers solicited companies that used a personal name. Sutherland says, "Wherever we ran, I always made a point of getting to the media. I told them, 'If I didn't have Archie Hackwell Construction Ltd.'s support, I wouldn't be here.' I always had a good rapport with the media, and I started to get a ton of press."

When Kelly Sutherland began racing in 1969, chuckwagon drivers received paltry sponsorship and negligible prize money. He recalls, "I viewed all the old wagon drivers as my folk heroes, but it always upset me that they never ever had enough profile. You could ask anyone in Calgary if they knew the Glass name. They certainly did, but driver Ron Glass never used it to his advantage, financially, or raising the sport to where it should be." Sutherland felt that if the drivers properly marketed themselves, they would be valuable to companies. His personal ambition became clear: whenever people mentioned "Kelly Sutherland," there would be only one thing that came to mind — chuckwagon racing.

Sutherland perceived many opportunities to promote himself. He says, "The first time I ever saw a poster of a chuckwagon driver was in 1970. Do you know where that came from? I made it. I sat outside of the High River grandstand and signed autographs at a table. It wasn't really accepted by other drivers, but to my astonishment, people just lined up."

In 1979, the Calgary Stampede increased the profile of corporate sponsorship and raised the level of investment by introducing the annual tarp auction. Each March, four months prior to the Rangeland Derby, buyers bid to place their names on the tarps for the duration of the ten-day Stampede. Thus, amidst the powerbrokers of Calgary's business world, the cowboys place their reputations, personality, and driving records up for auction. Beer is offered prior to the auction, lubricating bidders and their wallets.

The auction has proven to be extremely popular and helpful to the cowboys' finances. The concept of tarp auctions has become so successful that the separate chuckwagon associations also hold auctions for the shows on their circuits. The Calgary Stampede tarp auction is held in March, and the associations' auctions take place in April. Depending on their business and where their customers live, the Calgary sponsors may or may not also purchase the tarp for the tour shows.

Nevertheless, Calgary is where the big money remains. Two thousand people crowd into the Archie Boyce Pavilion and into the neighbouring Round Up Centre saloon to watch the auction on closed-circuit television. People line the stairways, staring at the cowboys. Large video screens above the stage replay footage of the drivers competing at the Stampede, and pyrotechnics flare up around the auctioneer, inflaming bidding. Each cowboy walks alone onto the stage. He stands facing the audience, with the Stampede Queen or one of the Stampede Princesses as his chaperone. Amidst the machine-gun patter of the auctioneer, and the "Yah's" of the bid catchers, the disarmed and unsure cowboy waits to see how much he will sell for.

Nevada describes how it feels to have his abilities up for sale. "When you walk in there, you feel like a cow in an auction market. My first year auctioned off, the Stampede's mascot, Harry the Horse, kept running out and bugging me. 'Back off, eh!' It's tough. You don't know what people think of you. You're wondering how many people are there to bid, or how many think it is a waste of time to lift their hand on you." He continues, "I'm watching the bidders, the ones who I don't know. I'm trying to figure out who the hell they are. With the cameras rolling, it's not that fun standing on stage. If you talk to the drivers, their biggest worry is, 'What if I sell for the shits?' It's embarrassing to possibly not even get a bid. Thankfully, I haven't had that trouble too much."

One of Buddy Bensmiller's long-time Stampede sponsors is National Tobacco, manufacturers and marketers of Copenhagen Chewing Tobacco. The company sponsored Bensmiller despite the fact that, unlike many cowboys, he does not chew tobacco. Bensmiller says, "I told them I'd pack a tin, but I won't chew it." He adds, "I've never had anybody come to me and ask, 'Why do you pack a sponsor whose product kills people?' My dad and mother both died from cancer. It's everybody's free choice as far as I'm concerned. Just because I'm packing the tarp, doesn't mean people should chew. [National Tobacco are] the ones paying my livelihood, but I still wouldn't chew for them and they don't expect it. It's been a good relationship."

At the 2000 Calgary Stampede canvas auction, Buddy Bensmiller's tarp was again purchased by National Tobacco to promote Copenhagen, for $120,000; Jim Nevada's tarp was taken by Fountain Tire, for $55,000; and Kelly Sutherland's tarp sold for a record bid of $165,000, to Sky Reach Equipment. The Calgary Stampede holds back a 20 percent administration fee from all these bids. A total of $1,653,500 was spent on Stampede wagon sponsorship at that auction.

The auction bids can be deceptive, though. Chuckwagon sponsorship is a maze of deal making. Although the tarp event is an auction, drivers may not actually earn what is reported. For instance, the drivers may negotiate deals in advance, so that no matter what the sponsor's final bid price is, they are paid a guaranteed amount. If the final bid is lower than the agreed price — for example, the deal is $100,000, but the final bid is $75,000 — the cowboy is still paid the higher amount, $100,000. If the final bid is higher — for example, the deal is for $100,000, and the cowboy sells for $150,000 — the driver is paid only $100,000, and the company saves $50,000.

Nevada adds, "Some guys make deals, and say, 'Let's run me up so I look good.' I never agreed with that. Other guys abuse deals to make them look like big shots. One driver sold for $100,000, when he only got $40,000. Why pay the extra twenty percent commission to the Stampede, just so you get your name in the paper? No one remembers it two days later. I don't understand that."

Some cowboys also need to watch that they do not put themselves forward as poor investments. "Some of these drivers have to learn to grab a brain," remarks Nevada. "Their barns are not well kept, there's not a good atmosphere, they're not very professional, and they've always got a hand out asking for more. Wagon committee members and drivers warn first-time sponsors to stay away from those drivers."

During the season, the wagon sponsors sometimes do not understand the cowboys' racing strategies. Nevada says, "At times drivers have to explain to their sponsors, 'I'm not going to do good at this show because I'm trying to get this other horse working before I get to Calgary.' That's where the prize money is."

Wagon cowboys depend upon the goodwill and generosity of their benefactors and often develop long-term sponsorship with companies that reflect their personalities and values. Nevada says, "I work well with companies who have started from scratch — like Fountain Tire outlet managers. They didn't have it handed to them, but they had to work to get there. The owners are down to earth, and they're not phoney."

Successful partnerships between sponsors and cowboys are based on common principles. The cowboys rely upon the sponsors' finances, and the sponsors count on the cowboys to admirably promote their products or services. The wagon community also acknowledges the sponsors by making a concentrated effort to buy products — be it home appliances or tires — from those businesses involved with the wagons. It is a symbiotic relationship.

Family and sponsors give cowboys the emotional, moral, and financial support they need. This essential backing inspires the cowboys to travel in the direction of their fears and hopes. The security of friends sees the cowboys through their doubts and pushes them on. They do not race alone.

The seventy-five-second chuckwagon race little reflects the cowboys' labours and their families' sacrifices. These are all behind the scenes. Buddy Bensmiller states, "You can't say we compete only to race, because the races are only a minute and a half — the rest is all work. The sport is something you've got to enjoy." The cowboys' bruises, the long hours, and even the wrinkles weathered into their skin are a result of their passion for those oat-fuelled engines. Bensmiller muses, "They all figure she come easy, but she definitely doesn't come easy."

Yet the cowboys keep following the grey asphalt highways to the next show. They are forever "hooked on wagons," and would not barter their lifestyle for any price. True to western lore, chuckwagon cowboys know they're rich, even when they're broke.

CHAPTER 3

A Bridled Love Affair

We do not force a horse to do anything he doesn't want to do. We can't win with a horse that doesn't want to win. My horses love to win. They know when they have won a race.

KELLY SUTHERLAND

Ask any chuckwagon cowboy and he will tell you flat out that his outfit's success is tied to his horses. No matter how urgently a cowboy pulls on the reins, it is the horses that ultimately determine the champion. The horses are the spirited partners on the track, the flexing muscle behind every victory, the soul of the sport.

The horses are unwilling allies — horses and cowboys train and work together toward a common racing goal. And like dogsled mushers, wagon cowboys develop a true partnership with their animals. The bond formed is an intimate one. From sunrise to sunset, the cowboys' first concern is their horses.

Chuckwagon cowboys aim to bring together and "tool" a harmonious team of horses. The horses will become a well-trained, interdependent, and high-strung family. But horses have as many different personalities as cowboys, and each cowboy works better with some horses than with others. So the cowboys must find horses that are compatible with one another, as well as right for their individual styles.

Because of their speed, gelded thoroughbreds are used exclusively in chuckwagon racing — both for pulling the wagons and for outriding. For three hundred years thoroughbred horses have been bred for their heat, their manic energy, and their drive to run. Originally developed in England — from Arab stallions — thoroughbreds are sensitive and high-spirited horses, and they possess slim, powerful bodies with broad chests. Kelly Sutherland states, "I love thoroughbred horses. I can't think of anything more magnificent."

All the thoroughbreds that are harnessed to wagons in fact begin their racing careers with jockeys on flat tracks. When the horses become unwanted, the cowboys purchase them for chuckwagon racing. Kelly Sutherland says, "My horse Brushfire Billy was the best two-year-old in British Columbia. He earned $186,000; but three years later I bought him for $1,200. His legs simply could not take the weight of a jockey. There were zero options left for the horse, yet he was still an incredible animal, very unassuming, not a big horse, not a splashy horse — but put together really well with solid conformation."

He adds, "There are thousands of these horses born every year, and they have got to have somewhere to go. People are shocked by the type of horses we have. Horses from California, Mexico, New York, Argentina — all work their way north to the wagons."

In wagon racing, the front two horses are referred to as the "lead team" or "leaders," and the rear pair as the "wheel team" or "wheelers." The addition of the figure-eight barrel turn makes wagon racing much more demanding than a flat race, and each horse's position requires different characteristics.

For example, the right-hand leader must be able to make an unnatural sharp right-hand turn at the top barrel, leading the entire team. Plus, once he is on the oval track, he and the right-wheeler are both always farther from the rail. If the two right-hand horses are not faster than the left-hand horses, they will pull the wagon away from the rail when it enters the curves, allowing pursuing wagons to take advantage of the rail position.

Furthermore, to make the barrel turns, the two leaders need quick feet (this is the same for rodeo's barrel-racing horses). Behind the leaders, the wheelers must love to run and must be robust enough to pull the bulk of the wagon's weight. And most importantly for the driver, both the wheelers and leaders have to respond willingly to the lines. There is no rider to coerce the horses — unlike in outriding — so manoeuvring and maintaining control are far more challenging.

As Kelly Sutherland sees it, a superior wheel horse is a horse with an unusual personality. He points out that since wheel horses can never win a race (they will always be outrun by the lead horses), they must have the right kind of attitude. "A good wheeler must be content getting dirt in his face for five-eighths of a mile." He adds, "A good wheeler needs to be aggressive physically and mentally because as he turns the barrels, he always gets the shit knocked out of him by the [wagon] pole."

The wagon pole is critical in linking the team of horses to the chuckwagon. The wooden or metal wagon pole extends straight out from the front end of the wagon and runs between the left-side horses and the right-side horses. Branching off from the wagon pole are two two-foot-long doubletrees, one at the front tip of the pole and one near the wagon. On each side of the doubletree, a short singletree is attached. Fastened to each of the four singletrees are a horse's tugs, which enable each horse to help pull the wagon's weight.

Sutherland continues on the subject of wheelers: "The wheelers are different individuals, particularly the right-hand wheeler. He is like a hockey goalie: he's way out in never-never land. He's totally off-the-wall all the time, he kicks once in a while, and has some quirks about him. Any good right-wheeler I've ever had has been like that. He just stands by himself."

Cowboys debate over which horse is most important to an outfit. Most select either one of the leaders. For example, Buddy Bensmiller, like many drivers, feels the right-leader is the vital horse, since that is the horse that initiates the decisive top turn, and the rest of the team follow him. Kelly Sutherland believes otherwise. He explains, "For me, I have an unorthodox turn of the barrels, and the smartest and hardest horse to find is the right-wheeler. Naturally, most drivers on the figure-eight pattern make a wide sweeping turn, but I go very, very close to the barrel. I go straight up, wide open, turn, and go straight back. My wagon actually stops dead for a split second on the long barrels. Since I go so close to the barrel, the right-wheeler has got to keep charging and pushing, even as I turn his head sideways and the [wagon] pole bangs him."

He details, "Most horses start to cheat after that pole touches them a couple of times. As soon as the pole is coming, they just stop and turn. Only twenty percent of the horses we buy can outride, ten percent can win on a wagon, and there is only a one percent turnout rate for a right-wheeler. The right-wheeler is a real brute for punishment. He is an outstanding running horse, a loner, and one who does not mind being rammed and pushed on. To find all those attributes is very difficult."

Surprisingly, outriding horses are also not easy to find. They must be fleet of hoof as well as have a calm disposition. "They are very hard to come by," Sutherland remarks. "Whereas a wagon horse is a hyper type of individual, an outriding horse is so lazy, hopefully he has enough energy to eat." This relaxed attitude is necessary prior to the starting gun, especially for the stove man, who may hold his horse's line with his teeth. Kelly adds, "That horse cannot move, cannot walk, and cannot push; the outriders need a horse they can control."

Sutherland adds, "Outriding horses pack 230 to 240 pounds, nearly double what they packed as a racehorse. During the race, the outriding horses trot around the barrels, and with no mistakes they can easily catch a wagon; but if the horses cause themselves a bit of trouble, then the outrider must ride like hell to catch up. Outriding horses need to be foolproof, since they can start cheating on themselves, knocking over barrels and taking shortcuts."

Jim Nevada considers, "People think 'a horse is a horse,' but the different personalities are amazing. I had a horse, Painted Indian, who hated Crazy Harold [a friend of Nevada's]. When he saw Harold, he started chasing him backwards, trying to kick him with his back hooves. The horses have personalities, just like people."

All year long, the drivers attempt to put together a smooth-running outfit, to unite four horses that will turn together and gallop in a singular, fluid motion. Yet no matter how athletically gifted some horses may be, they may not fit the team. Jim Nevada says, "It is like when your team's two best hockey players may not work together. You've got to figure out what horses work best. In the summertime, my mind never stops thinking up combinations. The more horses you get, the less sleep you get. All I'm thinking about is combinations and how to get them to work together better. It drives my wife nuts."

The horses require a significant investment, in terms of both time and money. Kelly Sutherland estimates that each horse annually costs him about $1,000 to keep, including feed, shoeing, and vet bills. He owns forty to fifty horses, which adds up to $40,000 to $50,000. The exorbitant price of maintaining a stable deters new competitors from entering chuckwagon racing and is another reason why family support is so necessary.

No matter how many horses the cowboys own, it is never easy finding the right horse for the right position. A few drivers, like Sutherland, have the finances or corporate sponsorship to buy horses already broken by other drivers. These horses can cost up to $20,000 each. But since there are not enough broken horses, and no horses are bred specifically for chuckwagons, each autumn and winter the cowboys truck to North American racetracks to buy used geldings. For the cowboys, it is a constant financial gamble. They spend thousands of dollars on horses without knowing how these horses will take to wagon racing.

Each cowboy shops for different characteristics in a wagon horse. Kelly Sutherland describes what he looks for when he buys a thoroughbred: "You need a gelding that's stout. The horse is no good unless he's four years old, not much good if he is past eight, and he should cost between $2,500 to $3,000." He adds, "I like to look at the horse's head: it'll give you an idea as to what type of horse it'll be — hyper, aggressive, or a pony. I also look for a responsive horse, one that's got a very tender mouth. I tend to drive with fingertip control, and I don't like to strong-arm horses at all. Any driver who turns tough has soft hands, and if I have a horse with a lot of mouth, he plays me out."

Buddy Bensmiller is constantly buying, breaking, and selling horses. He is an enterprising and fastidious horseman. To illustrate, in 1992 he bought fifty-six head of horses, searching for one left-leader. He still did not find the horse he sought. He says, "I used to buy other guys' horses, but I'm getting too old to work with everybody else's bad habits. If a horse is going to have a bad habit, I want him to have mine. I can work with that — that's why I never buy a broken horse."

When it comes to choosing horses, Bensmiller believes there is no guarantee of finding the "right" horse. No instruction manuals are delivered with the horse's personality. He says, "Guys will tell you they knew their horse would be a good one, but I'd like to know how. I've owned a thousand head, and maybe a half-dozen of the best horses in the business. It is still a lucky guess."

Unlike other wagon drivers, Bensmiller generally uses smaller thoroughbreds, fifteen to sixteen hands high. He says, "It doesn't matter how big a horse is, it's how big his heart is. I go by the size of heart they have inside of them."

Bensmiller also picks his horses based on the colour of their coats. He describes, "I'm now trying to buy black horses. Both my wagons are painted black, and I use white harnesses so it looks good. At one time I bought grey horses, and in 1989, when I won the Calgary Stampede, I had all greys. After I won, every time I went to the racetrack it was, 'Oh, you're the guy who wants grey horses,' and they upped the price by a thousand dollars, so I quit buying them."

He adds, "I could never imagine going to a sponsor and asking them to buy a horse I could not afford, but so many drivers do it. When cowboys offer me twenty thousand dollars for one horse, and I turn it down, people say I'm nuts. I say, 'Why? That horse cost me eight hundred dollars. If I start selling those kind of horses, my sponsors will get mad.'"

When the horses are brought home from the racetrack, they may find the new freedom on the farm unsettling. Some of the animals have lived most of their lives in a barn stall. Occasionally, the horses gallop right off, running flat out across the prairie, stopping only when they come upon the barbed wire fence.

At their ranch, Bensmiller and his sons continue to hitch and work with horses every day. In carrying out their chores, they have resisted succumbing completely to the temptation of machinery. In the winter, the Bensmillers use a team of horses to pull their hay-filled wagons, and in the summer, the cattle follow those same teams to new pastures. The family trains teams and saddle horses, and Buddy also offers many winter sleigh rides to the local community. Even when the thermometer reads thirty below, frost-covered Buddy and his sons can be found driving their horses.

Buddy says, "It did not used to be unusual for wagon families to break so many horses, but it is now. My sons have always been good about chores, and the outriding and the driving has always been their choice. I think the experience they get now will help them. I've always said that if I make them compete, they aren't going to do it anyway." Simply by working with horses so constantly, Bensmiller and his sons have gained a feel and a sense for horses that not all drivers possess.

Jim Nevada offers his opinion on what keeps Bensmiller successful, "You can tell the guys who are good with horses; they keep breaking new horses, working them in, and staying high in the standings. A lot of guys will get a good outfit going, and stop breaking horses. A good horseman will realize when they will peak, and bring new horses in." Nevada also agrees it is not easy finding a wagon horse. "It's just hit and miss. A lot of horses who have one or two racetrack wins turn out better than the ones who have twenty-five. Some of the biggest, ugliest, hammer-headed-looking things — they look more like a camel than a thoroughbred — can be the best ones. It is the size of heart that matters."

To advance the horses' training, the drivers also devise special feed diets. Nevada states, "It's no different from a person who runs marathons; there are certain foods the horses eat, making themselves feel better." Bensmiller, for example, has developed a winter feeding and a summer feeding schedule. He says, "I feed the horses hay in the winter to give them more 'bottom' in the summertime, more finish. I always used to have hard-barrelling outfits, enabling me to make it to the front, but coming home the guys started catching me. But when I feed winter hay, if I get behind or get in front, they usually won't catch me."

In the chuckwagon world, the key to the feed-mixture puzzle can be highly coveted. Bensmiller chuckles, "Everybody's got their own secrets. One guy at Meadow Lake was always around at feeding time, watching what we put in. At that time vitamin E came in a white powder, so he asked, 'What is that stuff?' I said,

'It's flour.' He asked, 'Why do you feed him flour?' I answered, ''Cause it tightens their shit; it tightens them up inside, and they can run faster.' By geez, I saw him later in the summer and his hired hands told me he was feeding his horses flour."

Despite the formulas they have come up with, the cowboys have discovered that keeping to the identical feed rations year after year does not always work. Nor does keeping to the same routine of how the horses are fed. Horses are unpredictable. Bensmiller enjoyed several years of continual success, but one summer, after having put out the same amount of hay and feed the previous winter, the horses seemed healthy but had no "run." The problem lay in how the feed was distributed. Bensmiller recounts, "They had an infection in their windpipe, caused from breathing in the hay dust flying up from the feeders. Now I just sit the hay on the field, and I haven't had any trouble since."

In the spring, the hearts of both cowboys and horses sing with optimism. Spring holds the fresh promise of the new racing season. It is also the time to break new horses and try out new horse combinations. The hope in the air is palpable.

At the end of March, chuckwagon training season begins in backyard fields and on self-ploughed tracks. This gives the cowboys the time to get their horses conditioned for the racing season, which starts in early June, and to ensure the horses will be at their physical peak for mid-July — all primed for the Calgary Stampede. To get their horses to compete at the highest performance level possible, the cowboys use various training strategies. These tactics can be trade secrets. Kelly Sutherland says, "All the cowboys will tell you a story on how they train, just sometimes it ain't true."

During training, the drivers work to remove the fear from new horses and teach them discipline. The harness, the noise, and the perceived threat of the ever-following wagon are all new to the animals. Kelly Sutherland can judge by the fifth or sixth time a horse is hooked up whether it has the necessary attributes to wagon race. He says, "If a horse doesn't like it, they quite soon figure out they can get away with a lot of shit — and one thing is not running. We use only lines attached to their bits, and no whips, so we have no way of disciplining them." Like the cowboys themselves, wagon horses either take to the sport naturally or do not.

Sutherland adds, "In spring training, our hands are completely bruised from stopping those horses trying to run away." All chuckwagon cowboys are also very careful to protect their hands, especially when working around sharp farm equipment and machinery. Sound hands and fingers are vital for wagon drivers — their fingers control their horses, through the subtlest touch on the lines.

Combined with proper springtime feeding, training encourages the horses to build up endurance and muscle mass. Sutherland stresses, "The object of training is to have the horse's lungs in shape for a half-mile race in thirty days, and in ninety days to have his body in shape. We try to build up muscle tone, to build up wind, [such as through] jogging." He adds, "It's pretty simple, except sometimes a horse can only take so much. Some love it, some don't. A horse who doesn't like training, and you keep training him, well he's going to show you he's not happy. Similarly, a horse who needs a lot of training, but is trained lightly, won't produce mentally or physically. The toughest part of training is figuring out those combinations of horses."

To build up their horses' muscle tone, both Sutherland and Bensmiller use a pickup truck as an exercise tool. Four compatible horses are hooked up to an attachment on the truck and led into a slow gallop. This allows the horses some equine cross-training. However, just as with feed diets, drivers differ in regards to training formulas, and Jim Nevada does not believe in truck training. Nevada prefers to first trot his horses around his home corral, and then hook them up to a wagon, trotting, cantering, and running them across his quarter-section property.

As the horses gain physical stamina, so do the cowboys. From regularly driving the horses and working the lines, the cowboys develop muscle mass in their shoulders, arms, and back. However, there is pain to this gain: the horses are fresh and keen, and their enthusiasm can result in strained and bruised muscles for the cowboys. Some springtimes, Kelly Sutherland's back has been covered in bruises from vigorously hauling back on the lines.

When Bensmiller breaks new horses to harness, he hooks them with a dependable work horse, perhaps a Clydesdale, and uses the work horse's leadership to teach. Buddy says, "If there is a wreck, the work horse will stand still while you get the young horse untangled." He adds, "A thoroughbred is a funny horse: if they get something in their head, it's hard to get it out. When I first break a thoroughbred, I like to go a fair speed, because he was never taught or bred to go slow. We'll go as fast as the old work horse will go. Then when he's comfortable to the harness, I'll hook him with other thoroughbreds. Once they settle into driving, I'll slow them up. If you do too much of the same thing, the horse gets sour and starts cheating on you."

Bensmiller suggests he has better luck than most cowboys keeping his horses together. "A lot of guys have horses lasting two or three seasons, but I've got horses that last for years. I think it stems from how you train and look after them." He believes today's new drivers do not have the same commitment to training. He states, "George Normand and I hitched up nine outfits every day in the spring. We had sixty-seven head of horses tied up in the barn. On the days we hooked the old-timers, it would be eleven outfits. Today's young guys don't do that any more, they have one or two outfits at the most, and if they don't feel like hooking them up, they put the horses behind a truck."

After fifty to sixty days of physical training, the horses are ready to practise at a local racetrack. "As soon as a thoroughbred sees a racetrack again," says Jim Nevada, "all of a sudden it clicks, and they remember, 'This is where I race. This is where we get dangling.' Once I'm back at the track, I start stopping and starting the horses, teaching them to start together as a team." Nevada describes how the cowboys get the four horses to start in unison: "Some guys use voice commands like 'Hep!' or 'Haw!', snap the lines, and punch 'er. Kelly holds the horses back, so there's pressure on the horses' bits, and when the horn goes he throws the lines at them, releasing the pressure. How you start them depends on how the outfit best responds."

Spring training ends with the first tour show. When the horses are harnessed to race, the drivers can soon tell how their horses feel physically and mentally, through the four lines. The lines, extending from the bits in the horses' mouths to the drivers' hands, serve as brake, accelerator, and steering wheel. Sutherland describes, "My present team has really soft mouths, and with hardly a pull on the lines I can pull them left or right."

Through this palmful of leather, the cowboys can sense what kind of run to expect. But the lines also disclose to the horses how the driver is feeling, whether he is relaxed or unsure. The communication is two-way. And depending on what the lines tell them, the horses will act accordingly. So the cowboys must exude confidence and control when taking the reins, for the four horses must be certain that to be first across the finish line is the most important thing in the world.

Sustaining this drive in the horses is one of the enigmas of wagon racing. It is something that happens away from the crowds; they can in the solitude of the barns. The horses can see into the cowboys; they can sense their expectations. The cowboys must impart confidence, encouragement, and leadership. The smallest tinge of doubt can whip through the outfit, and suddenly the horses have lost the assurance to surge ahead. Conversely, one determined horse can unite and impel the rest of the outfit into flight, including the cowboy. How the reins are handled, the cowboy's tone of voice, the energy he conveys — everything contributes. A winning outfit embraces ambition, conviction, and will.

When Jim Nevada first began driving, he knew he had some wild horsepower. He recollects, "When you start breaking your own horses, you throw in horses that maybe shouldn't be in a race. I don't know how many times I got fined for my firecrackers. One year I had a $2,500 fine for wagon interference from our board of directors. Well, they're all city guys who couldn't ride one horse let alone drive four, and they're coming over and giving me shit."

Nevada's fines were a regular joke at the World Professional Chuckwagon Association's year-end banquet. For several years, the master of ceremonies, Les McIntyre, announced, "We'd all like to thank Jim Nevada for putting in his fines, and paying for this year's banquet." Nevada says, "I was going to persevere, even if I had to work all winter to pay my fines. I was not going to lose to some city-slickin' tie-jockey. The officers are good for the business side, but I don't know why they're allowed to give fines. They don't know a cooper from a hame strap."

Nevada's wild driving experiences strengthened his abilities. He discovered which types of horses he worked with best and gained the techniques to manoeuvre overly ambitious and rebellious chargers. He feels his learning curve took longer than most, but it gave him a broader teamster education.

After years of handling horses, Kelly Sutherland can pick out the changes in his horses' moods. Sutherland says, "The horses do not understand if they knocked a barrel over or how fast they were, but they want to win the race. They know whether they won or not." He gives an example: "One race, I wasn't going to make the rail, so I turned and pulled in behind another wagon and gave the horses an easy trip. That meant I could go right back out the next night, and the horses would run just as hard or harder. After the race, Ralph [Sutherland's left-leader] was mad. He tried to run away all the way back to the barn. He just shook his head, grabbed the bit, and tried to run away. Ralph can just about talk to you when you're driving." Kelly adds, "Out of two thousand head of horses, Ralph is the best horse I've owned." ("Ralph" is the nickname for his horse Prairie Premier, named after Alberta premier Ralph Klein.)

Continuing on the topic of his horses' dispositions, Sutherland notes, "When I win a race I always pat a horse very strongly on the chest, right between the front legs, and on the side of the neck. They're accustomed to being rewarded that way at a racetrack. Those horses just explode. If I have a really good race in Calgary,

I'll take the bridle off, pat them, and they just beam. They know, especially the leaders, that they've won."

Working with so many horses, these cowboys encounter all types of equine temperaments and personalities and behaviours. And if there is one thing most horses do well, it is hurting themselves. Every cowboy faces the costs and the effort needed to keep a healthy stable. Yet more than time and money are at stake: there is the cowboys' compassion for their fellow teammates.

Bensmiller shares, "Our horse Dooley was bucking and playing. One time, it had just rained a little. It was muddy, slick on top, and somehow the little bastard went up in the air and landed on his side. He tried to get up and couldn't, so I ran over and got a hold of him. I finally got him up, but he started running backwards and down he'd go again. I loaded him up and ran him to the veterinary hospital in Saskatoon. They x-rayed him and the vet said, 'This horse's neck is broken. He shouldn't be alive.' He showed me the x-rays, and there was a hairline fracture. I asked, 'What do I do with him?' and the vet said, 'Can him.'"

Buddy continues, "Every time Dooley bent down to eat he'd pinch his nerves and flip over backwards, so I asked, 'What if I take him home and tie his hay and water so he doesn't have to bend down?'" So Bensmiller took Dooley home and put him in a box stall. For two months Dooley's food and water were set high in the air. Dooley became very thin on a diet of only hay and water, but he healed and gamely returned to race.

Not all horses are as loved as Dooley. The cowboys do cuss and choose their favourites. Nevada remarks, "Some you just hate their guts, but they're such good horses you've got to keep them. They step on you, push you, run you over, or break something; but you've got to put up with them because they're the best. But some are the best, and they're great to be around."

Around the barns, Kelly Sutherland's competitors speculate as to what he does to his horses so that they give him such consistent success. Sutherland answers, "I work with my horses over and over till it feels comfortable. Like a human, horses will only perform their best when they feel comfortable or at ease." He says, "Even if I was drunk, I'd go to the stalls at 11:30 p.m. and fluff up the straw for the horses. If you watch horses in a corral, they'll fluff up their bed if they're going to sleep. If a horse is sound, it will sleep standing up or laying down, but most wagon horses are a little sore, so they tend to like to lay down."

Sutherland also attends to his horses' mental health. At least twice during the Calgary Stampede, Kelly takes his horses for a walk in a different direction and allows them to eat some grass. For horses used to open corrals, it is boring to be constantly in the Stampede's barn stalls, and with a little variety, the horses are noticeably more focused. They regain the edge needed to win.

After possibly ten to fifteen years of wagon racing, the horses will be retired. Many wagon thoroughbreds race into their late teens, continuing to compete many years longer than most flat-racing horses. For the cowboys, retiring a horse is not an easy decision. Sutherland says, "Without those four horses there's no goddam way I could win anything, so you get really attached to them, especially the ones with character."

Nevada echoes Sutherland's sentiments, "I've got horses at home that aren't making me any money, but I've lived with them so long that they become like kids. They eat, lay and walk around. They're retired."

Some horses cannot adjust to retirement. The sudden lifestyle change is a shock for those horses. They cannot cope with year-round liberty in the pasture. Sutherland describes, "It's like taking a child and having him do the same job till he was fifty and then retiring, it would be a big adjustment for him." He adds, "If they're good enough to use them to train new horses in the spring, especially lead horses, we keep them around. Often, they get fairly old and stiff, between sixteen and eighteen years old. They've had so much pounding in their joints, they may be in a lot of pain, and if they are, I send them to the cannery. It's probably the most humane."

Eventually, owing to old age or freak accidents, the horses are put down. For the cowboys, these are dark days. The horses are friends, they are partners, they are family. Nevada relates, "You never know what will happen to a horse. Some of my horses were fartin' around, playing in the corral, and another horse ran right into the side of Chip's leg and snapped it. I heard the snap, and Chip just stood there looking at me, pivoting around on that one leg. Chip had that 'help me' look, and it just tore me right up. My buddy, a vet, came over and took a look; the bone was blown right out the side of his leg. That was the end of Chip. He was just like a family pet, and for a week there it just bugged me."

Sutherland, too, has keenly felt that loss, but his anguish has been tempered by time and experience. He says, "When I lost Chicago Mike, one of my finest first horses, I was really, really upset. But you get a little older, things are born, things live, and things die. It's a reality. Nothing is immortal."

Despite the cowboys' and their families' unreserved love for their horses, every summer the chuckwagon community faces accusations from animal-rights activists that wagon racing is cruel to horses. These allegations receive added attention when there is a spectacular wreck at the Calgary Stampede. The eyes of the world are on Calgary each July; chuckwagon racing is the premier event; and sometimes horses are injured and die.

Jim Nevada describes why the wrecks grab the media's attention: "When there's a thirteen-hundred-pound wagon flipping through the air and people flying over horses, it's a little more wilder to look at than three horses and jockeys piling up on the backstretch. When we pile up, it's like stock-car racing, you've got major-league objects flying through the air."

These isolated images perpetuate a notion of wagon racing as a reckless sport. Nevada counters, "Chuckwagon racing isn't a Ben Hur race. We don't pay four or five thousand dollars for a horse and try to kill it. You don't win money if you don't take care of your horses. We're drug tested, both us and the horses. Those horses would be in a dog-food can or on a plate in France, if it wasn't for wagon racing."

Yet the cameras record the accidents, and the sport is branded as brutal and insensitive. The media provide fodder for the activists' misunderstandings. Kelly Sutherland responds, "A horse off the racetrack has two choices: they're either going to a killing plant — 'the can' — or on to a chuckwagon. You ask that horse what he would want to do? What would he say?"

When chuckwagon cowboys talk about horses going to "the can," they are referring to the cannery in Fort Macleod, Alberta. Claude Bouvry, of Bouvry Exports, states that 50,000 horses are processed through this cannery each year. The horse meat is distributed around the world. Sometimes cowboys have bought horses waiting literally in the cannery's corrals, and then went on to train them into superb chuckwagon horses.

Sutherland adds, "I never ever have a problem with people confronting me about cruelty, because I know damn well if that horse could talk he'd tell me what he'd want to do. You drive to Fort Macleod, and they've got eight thousand horses waiting to be slaughtered in the feed lot. I'll guarantee if those horses could, they'd trade goddam positions anytime. They're not mares, so they cannot be bred. There's no other alternative for those old geldings. I'm not against slaughtering horses because at least there's a market for them. If they're not used and they can't be fed properly, then that's the place for them."

Bensmiller concurs with Sutherland, "Why aren't those horses for sale? It is because they can't run any more, and they're not making a living at the racetrack, so they have to be sold. Ninety-nine percent of these horses would be dead if it wasn't for wagon racing."

Thoroughbred horses are athletes, and the cowboys provide them with optimal health care, feed, and rest. Sutherland describes, "Running is all a thoroughbred knows. His pedigrees and breeding lines are based on it. After we break a horse onto a chuckwagon, he is used twenty-five to thirty trips [races] a year. He's turned out in August, back on to grass. Then in my instance, in October, he's back on self-feed grain until March, when I bring him in again for training. You tell me he doesn't love it? There's no argument."

Sutherland knows the boundaries of the sport. "I'm not saying there isn't a risk there for a horse dying or being injured, but statistics prove we injure and destroy way less horses than they do flat racing, by far. The only thing is our wrecks are spectacular and we are a spectator sport, whereas horse racing is a gambling sport. When you see the horse ambulance go out during a flat horse race, that horse ain't going just for a little x-ray."

Naturally and justifiably, the public is concerned about the horses' well-being. People have a fondness for horses and admire their sensitivity and gentle grace. When a horse is hurt, everyone feels like a traitor to the horse's trust. Wagon racing becomes an easy target.

Jim Nevada speaks in the sport's defence: "City people have different attitudes towards animals compared to the farm people. The way these animal-rights people are, they don't go behind the scenes, and yet they know all about it. You have a big wreck and suddenly every animal-rights activist is an expert on wagon racing, but if you ask them if they've been to the barns or how many horses go to 'the can' each year, they don't know squat. They're ignorant about it, but they're also experts about it. That's the biggest thing that drives me nuts."

Bensmiller echoes, "People don't understand. They need to come and see how the horses are treated, where they would be. I bought one old grey horse when he was five years old, I raced him till he was nineteen, and I finally put him down when he was twenty-seven. The vet told me when he was seven years old he wouldn't live another year. Even when he had cancer and lumps all over, that old bastard would buck and play." Bensmiller adds, "It makes me upset when people say, 'Your horse is this,' or 'Your horse is that.' Shit, my horses get better looked after than my kids."

The entire wagon community works to ensure the horses are well looked after. The responsibility is regulated and maintained by the wagon associations, the race committees, and also the drivers' peers. Bensmiller says, "I don't care what horse sport you're in, there are some people who are going to look after their horses better than others. We've definitely got guys that don't feed, but our association stays on top of them. If their horses are too thin, we send them home and penalize the cowboy with fines. It's my livelihood, and I'm going to look after the horses."

Bensmiller recalls one year in Cheyenne when the race organizers and cowboys were expecting some trouble: two or three busloads of activists were expected at the barns. Bensmiller relates, "They doubled the security around our barns. I asked one security officer, 'What are they going to do?' He said, 'They'll turn your horses loose.' I said, 'I thought these were the sons of a bitches who wanted to protect our horses.' He replied, 'They think they are doing the horses a favour by turning them out on the track.' Unreal."

On the other hand, animal-rights advocates have succeeded in raising the level of horse care in chuckwagon racing. Over the last couple of decades, the concerns raised by the activists have inspired both the general public and the cowboys to place more emphasis on the horses' well-being. The activists' challenges, combined with public pressure, has forced the wagon cowboys to more strictly monitor their animals' health. In front of the stadium crowds, and at ranches, there is less and less tolerance for those individuals who still hold antiquated ideas about animals and unreasonable expectations for them. Horses are no longer looked upon as slaves. Cowboys have been educated, and they, and especially their horses, owe a thanks to the animal-rights voices.

Nevertheless, if the animal-rights crusaders want vocal and strong-minded allies, they should now enlist wagon cowboys as their partners. The cowboys, who work constantly with animals and rely upon them so profoundly, have an intimate and frank appreciation of an animal's right to a meaningful life and death. If both sides can let go of the divisive fighting, they can join together to denounce those who continue to manage animals through fear, aggression, and pain. Then all will benefit, especially the horses.

Amongst the hundreds of horses in wagon racing, a select few are celebrities. Blessed with talents not shared by their peers, these horses are a rare privilege for a cowboy to own and drive.

"The top outfits are like the Lemieux's and Gretzkys of hockey," describes Sutherland. "They just live and breathe the sport. They love it. You can tell with the attitude they bring towards it. They're athletic and smart enough to figure the game out, whereas the other horses just don't have that natural ability." For instance, Sutherland considers his first team and his team of the late 1990s to have been the two best outfits he has ever had. Included in that first team was Chicago Mike, the first horse Sutherland owned. Kelly says of Chicago Mike, "He was a real goofball. If you looked him square in the eyes, you'd see one eye was about a half inch lower. He was just a little off-centre."

Sutherland received Chicago Mike when the horse was three years old. And within two years, says Sutherland, "he grew into the most powerful thoroughbred ever. He adapted to and loved the sport." Kelly adds, "At the time, he could've been the best horse on the grounds, but I didn't know how to drive. I was just a kid. You don't understand how good those horses are, until you don't have them." With Chicago Mike, Sutherland won all the major shows, except Calgary. Sadly, Chicago Mike died before Sutherland won Calgary, after breaking his hip in a freak barn stall accident.

Jim holds the lead down the backstretch at the Calgary Stampede, July 12, 1999.
(CAROL AND PAUL EASTON, WAGON PHOTOGRAPHY)

Jim races for home with a sizeable lead at Lethbridge, Alberta, June 17, 1999.
(CAROL AND PAUL EASTON, WAGON PHOTOGRAPHY)

Jim nears the finish line in front of the grandstand at the Calgary Stampede, July 14, 1996.
(CAROL AND PAUL EASTON, WAGON PHOTOGRAPHY)

PREVIOUS SPREAD: Jim on the homestretch at Grande Prairie, Alberta, June 4, 1999.
(CAROL AND PAUL EASTON, WAGON PHOTOGRAPHY)

Buddy shakes it at 'em around the third corner at the Calgary Stampede on July 13, 1997.
(CAROL AND PAUL EASTON, WAGON PHOTOGRAPHY)

PREVIOUS SPREAD: Buddy makes a social call on Troy Dorchester while racing at Hayworth Stables, outside of Strathmore, Alberta, on June 6, 1998.
(CAROL AND PAUL EASTON, WAGON PHOTOGRAPHY)

Buddy hugs the rail around the third corner at Lethbridge, Alberta, June 8, 1999.
(CAROL AND PAUL EASTON, WAGON PHOTOGRAPHY)

Buddy poses in 1997 with his World Championship Trophy and outriders Dale Gray and Wayne Wright. (ANGUS OF CALGARY)

Bensmiller agrees that there are special horses. He says, "There are only a few horses that can win Calgary, I don't care what anyone says. There's guys who get lucky and pull it off, but to do it year after year, that luck is not going to be with you. You need four horses that are going to click." And Sutherland reflects, "I believe when a horse becomes a superstar in chuckwagon racing, you have fulfilled something for them like no tomorrow. You've done a huge favour for that horse."

Yet no matter how extraordinary these horse may be, they are not immune to luck's fickleness. Bensmiller says, "Many years we worked awful hard to get horses back to health, but then accidents, outriders, and stupid penalties cost us. You work all spring on a horse, and then it's clipped in a race. That's how quick it is. There's a lot of luck in this business."

Persevering against such disappointments, the cowboys optimistically keep working with their horses. And where there are horses, there is always a job to do: feedings to carry out, new horses to purchase, training programs to start. As Bensmiller states, "I do it all year: buying, breaking, and doctoring. I try to get old injured horses that would have been canned healthy again so they can run. For me, the horses are a lifestyle."

Horses are the lifeblood of chuckwagon racing. They are the sport's force and vitality. They also pull at emotions as only animals can. Says Jim Nevada, "I have twenty-seven pets in my pasture. Some of the old boys, you can pet them just like your dog when they come running up to you. When I lose one, it's just like losing the family dog. It hurts. You don't sleep at night; you just wish it didn't happen."

Nevada has an exceptional attachment to his four-hoofed friends. He emphasizes, "I have a great deal of respect for horses. I work with them every day, I am a part of them, I bond with them. We love these horses."

The tie that connects the cowboys and horses is felt in the heart and spirit. The cowboys depend upon the horses' skills for their families' livelihoods, and the horses depend upon the cowboys for the gift of racing. Chuckwagon racing reveals the fellowship between horse and man, as these true partners race for bragging — and neighing — rights.

CHAPTER 4

Galloping Pandemonium

A wagon race is just a controlled runaway. There's no way you can stop those horses. But you can steer them.

KELLY SUTHERLAND

A chuckwagon race seems careless and foolhardy, but each turn on the track is filled with uncanny skill and heart-beat decisions. Jim Nevada describes, "With that many people, trained horses, and talent working in such a confined area, wagon racing is an art form." The cowboys are equine artists, and the dirt is their canvas. Fear and risk are fashioned into guided pandemonium; divine talents never looked so much like hell.

Observe chuckwagon cowboys and you'll see their entire demeanour changes when they get on the wagon seat. The cowboys' eyes disclose their intensity. Wagon racing demands from them a vigilant communion with their horses, and complete physical and mental concentration. Rarely are mistakes painless in a wagon race, and the cowboys must be "on" — alert, analytical, and in control. Their horses, their competitors, and their egos are relying upon it.

When the cowboys' wagons lumber onto the racetrack, the miles of travel, injuries, and debts are forgotten. It is time for the cowboys to put their horses where their mouths are. It is showtime.

The horses jog with anticipation onto the track. Before each heat, the drivers are allowed one slow warmup turn around the barrels. "When I go in for the practice turn," Bensmiller says, "I watch my horses to see what they're thinking, how they're feeling. Depending on how they drive in, I can tell how they are going to start."

After completing their practice barrel turns, the wagons return from the right to line up. As seen in the diagram in the introduction, the wagon to the far left — the one on Barrel 4 — moves in first to line up the hubs of its rear wheels with the bottom barrel. Wagons on Barrels 3, 2, and 1 then follow. Bensmiller describes how he keeps an eye on his competitors as they pull in: "I watch other outfits going in to get the timing right, so I'm not too far ahead or behind them. People tell me they've yelled at me before the race, but I don't even hear the announcer, I just blank it all out. All I see are the horses."

Similarly, Sutherland makes certain he does not go in to the starting barrel too quickly or too slowly. He says, "A lot of guys want to come in, stop, and go; so they come in to the barrels last. My outfit needs a little bit of time to sit — about two seconds. If they sit much longer, then I'm in trouble." Sutherland is also scrutinizing his horses as he pulls in. "I watch the lead team, and I can tell what they're going to do, just by their actions. Horses have good and bad days; they're not quite as 'off' as a human, but they do have better days. If they are really on the muscle, I will have a super big run. I'll holler at the outriders, 'Okay, boys, we're going for the gusto this trip!'" Sutherland adds that he focuses on his lead team just before the start. "I need to have their heads in a certain position, otherwise I won't make a very good turn. I don't care if they are not standing quite perfectly, because a horse always follows its head."

The moment before the horn blows is the stillness in the eye of the hurricane. It is the moment when the cowboys surrender themselves to fate. The same experience is shared by bull riders as they wait for the rodeo chute to open, or dog mushers as they stare into the icy distance, about to release the snow hook restraining their sled. The men and animals are centred, the wagons and outriders are steady. There is no turning back.

Suddenly the klaxon growls, the horses lunge, and the race is underway. "Hyaw!" scream out the cowboys. The outrider steadying the lead horses jumps out of the way. The three trailing outriders pitch the tent poles and stove into the wagon. The wagons twist into the barrel turns. Sutherland emphasizes, "In the first two or three seconds I know whether I'm going to make a hell of a turn just by the momentum. My outfit just goes. They go together, gathering speed."

There are two ways of turning the top barrel. Some drivers make a "swoop": they drive wide to the left — out to the chalk line that is drawn in the dirt and that defines their lane — and then sweep around the barrel. The rationale behind this style is that the momentum of the horses and the wagon is not stopped; therefore, the outfit should be travelling double-quick when it gets back to the track. The other style, which Kelly Sutherland employs, is to go dead straight and very close to the top barrel. The drivers nearly jackknife their horses as they turn.

The drivers require agile hands as they circle the top barrel, since they must hastily collect the approximately three feet of line that becomes slack during the turn. The leather lines are fed back out to the horses once the outfits unbend out onto the track.

The most electrifying and riveting moment for the cowboys and spectators is when the wagons charge into the left turn around the bottom barrels and swing onto the racetrack. At that instant, the horses hit full stride — the pull and thrust is tremendous. The back end of the wagons can skid wildly to the right, as the horses dig into the track and surge forward. Nevada states, "There is amazing torque coming around the barrel." The horses' incredible energy galvanizes the fans.

This is also where most chuckwagon wrecks have happened. The momentum from the bottom barrel turn simply hoists the wagon up and over on to its right side. The driver loses control, and with the three other wagons fighting for space in tight quarters, mayhem can result.

Bensmiller suggests, "If you make a bad turn at the speeds we're barrelling, then you're going to upset. Drivers don't set up, they come too straight to the turn and then crank 'er. When I had my grey outfit, I was on two wheels almost every time I turned the top barrel. My left-hand wheeler had so much power, he straightened out after the turn and that ol' wagon just lifted up. Not too often that happens on the top barrel — it's usually on the bottom."

Some of the early chuckwagon tracks offered peculiar additional challenges. Sutherland recalls one of the obstacles he and his competitors cautiously avoided in Cloverdale, British Columbia. He says, "The bottom Barrel 3 was a power pole. They widened the infield, and left the pole in the infield. Son of a bitch, nobody hit that pole, I tell you."

The advantage that can be gained through the figure-eight turn inspires Bensmiller. "That's where the excitement really is. I always had barrelling outfits [horse teams that cover the figure-eight barrels hastily], and I've always shot for barrelling outfits. I hate coming from behind. If you are out in front, the other drivers are running at you."

The cowboys attempt to be first off the barrels when they clear their figure-eight turns. Generally, the prize is the coveted rail position. The closer the wagons are to the rail, the shorter the distance the horses have to run to reach the finish line. Plus, being the lead wagon means a cowboy has less dust to eat and his horses are less likely to get cut. When outfits must drive between wagons to try to get to the front of the pack, the cowboys run the risk of their horses' legs being nicked by wagons.

Sutherland describes coming around the barrels: "There's always a lot of strategy. By the time I turn the top barrel and get to the bottom to take a look, I'm making adjustments. For example, if you're on the outside, and it looks like you can daylight somebody [take the lead], then you 'shake it at 'em.' If not, then you're making decisions quick."

Leaving the infield, the outfits face the five-eighth-mile race around the oval track. It consists of four turns, the backstretch (the straight stretch between the second and third turns), and the homestretch.

Sutherland states, "If I've made a big barrel turn, I try to get the engine and get the front end. If I'm turned out three wagons wide, I pull on my lines all the way until I can get back in and follow somebody. If I stay three wide, I'm going to get blown out the back end. I might hang two wagons wide, depending on who's next to me."

Coming into the racetrack's second turn, describes Kelly, "you're still following through from your move on the first turn. Then in the backstretch, I always try to give the horses a breather, especially if I'm at the front end or running in there tight, so they've got something left for home."

As the pounding mass of outriders and wagons comes around the third turn, the drivers estimate how much "run" remains in their team of horses. Depending on their wagon's positioning, the drivers may then haul back on their lines, giving their horses a brief chance to regain their wind. The drivers are also checking over their shoulders, looking for their outriders, deciding if they need to slow down slightly to let their outriders catch up.

After the fourth (and final) turn, the drivers pick a lane on the homestretch and the outfits hurtle toward the finish line. Bellowing and hollering, the drivers shake their lines at their horses. Nevada says, "The biggest adrenaline feeling is when you nose another team out at the finish line." He adds, "When you win, or when you come around the third turn and you know you've got lots of run left, those are the two good feelings in a race."

At the Calgary Stampede, more than 20,000 people are cheering and screaming as the wagons race neck and neck to a photo finish. Kelly Sutherland says, "In the race, you hear the roar of the crowd, but you can't hear anything the announcer is saying. You're so focused." There is so much kinetic energy that even the crowd seems to give a collective sigh, catching its breath, once the wagons thunder by.

Since the drivers cannot hear the announcer in the din of the race, they may be racing vigorously to the finish without realizing that a damaging penalty has already befallen them. For example, Sutherland notes, "A lot of guys, they drive hard coming to the wire, but then they glance into the infield and see their barrel is down. Unless an outrider has come up in the race and admitted he knocked over the downed barrel, they're kind of shocked."

Once past the finish line, the drivers promptly wrap their lines around their wrists and hands, and rein in their team. The zealous thoroughbreds keep running until past the second turn before the drivers can finally slow them to a jog. Each wagon race is physically exhausting for the drivers, yet their horses are still seething. Therefore, once the horses are slowed to a trot, an assistant jumps into each wagon to help with the lines.

The wagons then return to make their post-race parade in front of the grandstand — the cowboys acknowledge the fans — and they rattle back to the barns. The muddy wagons are hosed off, and the horses, still hot from the race, are cooled down, either by letting them run loose in temporary corrals or by leading and walking them around the barns.

As the horses calm down in their stalls, the cowboys may be heard whistling in the barns. Whistling induces the horses to urinate. When the thoroughbreds were at the racetracks, they were trained to give urine samples at the sound of whistling. After the wagon races, some horses may remain anxious and reluctant to urinate, which can lead to illness, so the cowboys purse their lips and whistle.

The wagon cowboys then make sure the horses are fed and watered, and that any race injuries are tended to. The crews are usually busy till nearly midnight. Finally, with the horses settled down, the cowboys and their barn crews can then take their break. They rehash the evening's races, comparing stories and strategy perspectives.

In preparing for a race, drivers brew their tactics hours, days, and even months beforehand. One scheme is to train separate teams of horses to perform better from specific barrel positions. For example, some teams are swift around the barrels, allowing the drivers a shot at the rail position; other teams are runners and can overtake other wagons down the homestretch. The cowboys make use of the varying strengths and abilities of different horses and different teams of horses.

Jim Nevada explains, "Every heat is different. You know which drivers you're hooked up against, so you're guessing what horses they'll hook up and what horses you should rest. For example, if you are on Barrel 4 and have a fifty percent chance of out-turning the others, then you'll hook quick-starting horses to give you that extra jump to the first barrel turn. If it's a 'tuck and follow game' — you know you won't be first off the barrels, but you could catch them on the track — then you hook horses who will still have some run on the turn home."

In contrast, Buddy Bensmiller tries to train his horses so they are adept off any barrel position. He says, "Some guys have outfits that will work on short barrels, some guys have outfits they figure work better on long barrels. When I'm in Calgary, I hook my best horses every night; they'll come off any barrel. I try to get the right training into my horses so they can last the whole ten days. If it looks like I'm going to get to the finals, then I'll give my team the night before off."

To be successful repeatedly requires planning ahead. Kelly Sutherland describes his strategy, "I draw the Stampede out like a road map. I've got ten days mapped out, and I can tell if my horses are getting stronger, or whether they're getting tired. The first five days I just want to run there, and let everybody else have all the trouble they're going to have. That will eliminate those guys who eliminate themselves. From the fifth or sixth day on, I get my ducks in a row and start getting ready."

At the Calgary Stampede, it is only the top four cowboys at the end of the ninth evening who race in Sunday's $50,000 final race. These are the outfits with the lowest aggregate, or combined, times after their nine heats. "Near the end of the week," suggests Sutherland, "if you get bumped out of the top four, you're much more dangerous, terribly dangerous. You've got nothing to lose, and you're going to take the utmost trip from those horses, while the top four guys are approaching everything with a little bit of caution."

To identify the faculties needed to win a wagon heat, one need look no further than Sutherland. The King's capacity to analyze an upcoming race is a key element of his success. He is a master strategist. Bensmiller states, "Kelly's the toughest. Other guys are tough, but I don't worry about them because the driving ability and knowledge isn't there."

In the morning before a race, Sutherland visualizes the race's possibilities, concentrating especially on the first fifteen seconds. He predicts how the race will evolve by evaluating his competitors' patterns. As with drivers of cars, some wagon drivers are more aggressive, some are more defensive, and some are willing to take chances. By studying his opponents, Sutherland predicts how they will respond during the race. He says, "In thirty years, I've probably been around the track fifteen hundred trips, and I've seen every different kind of scenario, every kind of wreck, knocked over every barrel, piled up, and went upside down."

Perhaps among Sutherland's most significant achievements is his ability to "seize the moment." He describes, "A lot of times in chuckwagon racing, it's a game of intimidation. People are quite threatened by me, and justifiably. They've got to have their hammers cocked if they're going to outrun me on any given day, on any given barrel. A lot of times I'll catch people when they're not concentrating as deeply as they should be."

And Sutherland does not shy away from challenges. "If I'm on a short barrel, I try to out-turn everybody. A number of drivers have difficulty turning Barrel 4, and they're always, always going to pull in behind. Only a few guys will try to make the front end off the short barrel." To make the rail position from Barrel 4 is risky. Kelly explains, "You need horses that have a ton of early gas, a tremendous start and charge. In the first two hundred yards, a lot of guys can't feed slack in their lines fast enough; their hands aren't soft enough, and if you miss it, you'll get hung out wide. You'll find yourself so far behind that they'll have to turn the lights on, waiting for you to get home. It's a gamble."

Sutherland also tells his horses whether or not they should try for the rail position. "I talk to the horses through the lines," he says. "They know whether or not they're going for the front end just simply by how I feather the lines to them. They have a tendency to go to the rail, but I have got to clear everyone's wagons in the infield, otherwise I'm going to cause some trouble and some penalties."

Throughout the race, the drivers are constantly calculating not only how to win but also how to avoid a wreck. Chuckwagon drivers do not want wrecks; they want to win a clean race. So the drivers pay attention to their competitors' driving habits. Bensmiller explains, "Like a good hockey player, you've got to read the play. It's not so much driving for myself; you've got to drive for everyone else. You know the guys you're with. Some of the guys are good drivers, and if there is a problem, you know it's an accident they can't avoid. Other guys are a wreck waiting to happen, so you're driving for them as well."

He emphasizes, "If you see a wreck coming, you've got to drive out of it. Most guys, all they do is pull on their lines . . . well, there are no brakes. You can pull all you want and the horses will still run a half of a mile on you. The best thing is to try and drive out of a wreck, but that's experience. You've got to be in control at all times if you're going to be on top of this sport."

In the early days of chuckwagon racing, track maintenance — or lack of it — also added to the wildness of the races. At many of the smaller tracks, the dirt was not hosed down adequately, and consequently dust was a constant problem. The cowboys drove blind as moles. Sutherland remembers, "There were no water trucks, and if you were following behind in a race, you drove into a wall of dust. You could see nothing. You piled up into guys who'd piled up."

And with alcohol added to the mix, the races justifiably earned the title of "The Half Mile of Hell." Some of the initial wagon teamsters lived up to the boozing and brawling cowboy reputation. But Sutherland notes how the sport has evolved, "The wild western, fighting, drinking type of people were a major part when I joined, but no longer." Nevada agrees, "By the sounds of it, thirty years ago, one out of two drivers were drunk. They had a mickey in the hay bunk. It was the Wild West. They raced, they drank, they fought, and the next day they were friends."

Today, stringent controls are in place to test drug and alcohol abuse on the track. "Alcohol is no longer a problem." says Nevada. "We and the horses are drug tested. It's too quick out there. If anybody saw someone else drunk, they'd go tell the officials, because you don't want to race against somebody who's been drinking. Everybody likes to sit around and have a beer and bullshit after the races, but I don't think drinking is a problem at all on the track."

Before Breathalyzers and regulations were commonplace, wagon cowboys sometimes resorted to their own "frontier justice." Years ago, one driver was downright uncordial to the rest of the cowboys. To rectify his disagreeable personality, the cowboys hammered horseshoe nails up through his seat. "Horseshoe nails are sharp and pointed, almost like a needle," explains Nevada. "The cowboy drove his rig over to the races, he sat down, and three or four of these nails stuck him in the ass. He bellowed, and his horses took off."

The potential for collisions still exists, however, and dilemmas do develop. A driver can get into a "hole": his wagon and horses are trapped by a wagon in front and a wagon on the outside. It is a tense situation. The cowboy needs physical strength and stamina to rein back his horses, slowing them so they don't run into the back of the lead wagon. With the outfits travelling at forty-five miles per hour, there can be quite a spill, especially if the cowboys are using frightened and panicky new horses. Unless his competitors are gracious enough to let him out, the cowboy is in a perilous bind.

To open a needed exit, a cowboy will shout at the other drivers. Even amidst the racket of wagons and horses, the cowboys can hear their competitors. Friendly patter and arguments both take place mid-race. Bensmiller laughs, "The odd time you have a visit. Sometimes they're friendly visits, and sometimes they ain't."

For a driver to win, he must have reliable outriders. The driver's achievements are bound to the skill and luck of his outriding crew. There is an unwritten contract between the driver and outriders. If an outrider fails to meet his responsibility, he will face the disappointment or even wrath of the driver. Outrider Jim Nevada has faced the fury of drivers and their wives when his outriding errors have cost his drivers a show. He nods, "Some weren't my fault, but it never comes out that way."

One year in Grande Prairie, Nevada was falsely accused of deliberately throwing the show, and he was threatened with being beaten up. He describes, "At the start of the race, my horse flipped his ass around, nicked our barrel, and knocked it down. Since it was behind me, I didn't even know he'd hit it. I threw the stove in, turned the top barrel, looked to the fallen bottom barrel, and thought, 'How the hell did that happen?'

"I got back to the barn and the driver came over to give me a lickin'. He thought I wanted someone else to win. He cussed me out. His wife cussed me out. Everyone cussed me out — and I had ridden as a favour. It's days like that you wonder why you outride."

The choice of outriders is up to the drivers. Bensmiller, Nevada, and Sutherland all have previous outriding experience, enabling them to better match outriders to their outfits. Jim Nevada explains, "After outriding, I understand [which] outriders are good with the leaders, who are better peg men, and who can't hold a five-gallon bucket. Some people prefer to drive a Volkswagen over a Mercedes — there are cars that suit people and horses that suit people. When you can do that, you eliminate penalties."

Sometimes it is particular horses who dictate where outriders ride. Nevada elaborates, "You always put certain outriders on horses who charge on their own to the top barrel, and they are always at the off-barrel peg [the tent peg on the wagon's right, farthest from the starting barrel]. Those outriding horses can lead themselves."

Outriders must be alert and work together, especially when there are four of them in an outfit. Nevada says, "If you're in the back throwing pegs, you've got to load them in unison or else the pegs won't go in — they're offset." The tent pegs are attached to the canvas flap, and if one goes in too quickly ahead of the other, they can whip themselves back out of the wagon. Nevada continues, "Sometimes, too, just before the horn blows, a horse will walk up behind you and actually put his head right on top of the tent peg. They make the tent peg hard to throw."

The barrel peg man (on the wagon's left and closest to the starting barrel) must also watch that he or his horse does not knock over the bottom barrel when he throws his tent peg. As well, he must make sure he does not accidentally run over the crouched stove man.

Once his tent peg is in the wagon, the barrel peg man waits until he is out of the stove man's way before jumping onto his horse. If the barrel peg man does not wait, and his and the stove man's horses are side by side, the stove man may become sandwiched between the horses, get knocked back down, and end up being late. Most outriders now wear running shoes, making it easier to run in the infield and to quickly jump up into the saddle without using their stirrups.

Sutherland agrees the proper collection of outriders is critical to his success. He says, "With my outriding crew, I only like to have one rookie, so the older guys can keep him on track. Every time I've won the Stampede, I've had a crew with lots of experience, so they don't make any mistakes. One year my stove man missed four times, so I hired the guy who could do it. That's when I started winning."

Of the four outriders, the stove man has the most unprotected outriding job. At the race's start, he is bent down low amongst the horses and the two peg men, since the rubber stove must be touching the ground. He is vulnerable, especially to his partners' rough pranks. Nevada relates, "As you throw the pegs in, you can hit the stove man right in the head with the bottom of the pegs. One year, I was riding for Roy David in Ponoka, and the first night — wham, wham — the peg men nailed me. They laughed. I was wearing a jockey helmet, but it still rocked me. Every night I kept bending down lower, trying vainly to avoid those pegs."

Outriders frequently play practical jokes amongst their own crew. Nevada chuckles, "Other times we put grease on the inside handle of a stove. Guys go up, grab the stove, and get a hand full of grease. Then they have a greasy hand to use to swing onto their horse."

The spirited outriders also make "social calls" in the middle of the race. Jim Nevada grins, "When we outrode in the slower heats, we used to do stupid stuff. For example, if a guy was a little overweight, we'd sneak up and squeeze his tummy rolls — geez, he'd almost jump off his horse. Other times the outriders passed around a pop or a smoke, or we'd carry squirt guns filled with cheap perfume. We'd squirt outriders or announcers on stage. There were always jokes being done."

It is not all fun and games for the outriders, however. Prior to the ten-pound rubber stoves, fifty-pound wooden ones were used. The stove man needed both hands to lift the stove, so he held his horse's lead shank with his teeth. Nevada has felt the repercussions of employing this tenuous bite. "There are a few of us outriders who have lost our teeth. Ninety percent of the time the driver did not tell us he had taken an old chuckwagon horse and put a saddle on him. When that horse hears the horn — poof — away he goes and away goes your teeth."

In one race, Nevada's horse bolted away, but a knot in the line was caught in Jim's mouth. Nevada details, "The top part of my skull was busted from my eye socket down to my mouth. It took nineteen stitches to put my gums together. One tooth was completely gone and the others were just dangling by their roots — but I finished the race."

To survive as an outrider requires a special brand of courage. Unlike racehorse jockeys, outriders must dodge thirteen-hundred-pound wagons; and unlike the chuckwagon drivers, the outriders have no security from a wagon box. They ride at the mercy of their horses and the wagons whizzing around them. It is an organized maelstrom, and it is no Sunday picnic.

The outriders' nerves really start jangling when a wagon goes down in front of them. Nevada relates, "At one wreck, Jim Shields and I were riding beside each other. We saw the wreck coming, and faded outside. The wagon went down and we missed it. Two young kids riding twenty feet behind us, who had more of a chance to get out of the way, were still in the jockey position, with their heads tucked down, when they ran into the wagon. No one was hurt, but I told them to get their heads out of their asses."

The wagons have the right-of-way during a race. The outriders are vulnerable to the drivers, and there can be close calls. Nevada says, "The odd time outriding, I've had to ride the rail — between the rail and a wagon. Some drivers don't let you go through there.

One guy ran me so tight I had red paint and grease on my ankle from the hub of his wheel. He was so close, a piece of rebar sticking out from the wheel's hub burnt a hole in my sock.

"An outrider must be able to ride a horse out there," Nevada emphasizes. "There have been a few fights because somebody cut somebody off, almost putting them under a wagon. It's a team sport, and you've got to open holes for guys. In the old days they used to cut each other off. There were a lot of games out there, but that was when you just outrode for one or maybe two outfits."

Today, with outriders working for many different drivers, they race together just as often as they ride for competing outfits. Nevada was the last outrider to ride in all nine heats, all ten days, at Calgary. His experience speaks, "You've got to work with the other outriders. Someday you might be in a pickle and need a hole, and that outrider will come back and help you, or they should, unless they are a total asshole, which has happened too." And on that point he adds, "Some outriders don't care who gets a penalty as long as they don't. They will even run over their own teammates to make sure that they're not late."

The ability to work together and carry out their roles is what drivers are looking for in their outriders. Nevada concludes, "If I didn't think my outriders knew their job, they wouldn't be riding for me. My job is the four horses pulling, not the four that are following. That's why the outriders get paid, and if they're not good enough, they'll be out of there real quick."

The persistent image of chuckwagon racing as the Half Mile of Hell perturbs Buddy Bensmiller. He says, "I cannot figure why you would call it that if you were having fun doing it. I suppose years ago, anything went. Stories are told of cowboys paying the lead outriders to hold their opponents' horses at the barrels, but the sponsors' arrival has changed the sport a lot. Nobody can look bad in front of a sponsor; no cowboy wants a bad image."

Regardless of how chuckwagon racing is depicted, it is still a western sport that has not lost any of its suspense and sense of impending calamity. A chuckwagon race remains a ranch cook's recipe for misadventure: thirty-two horses and twenty cowboys speeding at forty-five miles per hour on an enclosed track. Each race is a stomach-churning concoction.

Yet for the cowboys, it is a calculated game. Their training, their confidence in their horses, and their strategies equip them with a boldness tempered with skill. It is a contest of determination. They play the match with courage and coolness, intent on putting some envy in their competitors' eyes.

CHAPTER 5

The Competitive Edge

It was shocking for me to discover that a lot of people don't like confrontation. It doesn't bother me one bit. Sometimes you have to be a little confrontational to get your message across.

KELLY SUTHERLAND

Shaded under their straw cowboy hats, the cowboys wear a competitive intensity. Viewed from the grandstand, the cowboys are hardened, stoic, and uncompromising. They personify the classic cowboy image, as stereotyped by actor Clint Eastwood, of fearlessness and resolute spirit. They "Cowboy Up!" — there is no second place.

Pro wagon cowboys are like any world-class athletes — to become a champion requires the "killer instinct." The mental aspect is a huge part of a cowboy's ability to win. The top drivers are the ones who are psychologically geared up; they are ready for any "mental barrel." When the wagon cowboys are at their best, everything falls into place. Decisions happen automatically. They are in the "zone."

Bensmiller, Nevada, and Sutherland are systematic in their approach. Their equipment and horses are inspected for soundness, and they plan for everything. As best they can, nothing is left to chance. When something does go wrong, they have developed a contingency plan. Through practice and experience, these cowboys have learned what to do when a problem erupts and are prepared to steer their luck and skill.

Even when they are prepared, this very tense sport often strains the cowboys' nerves and emotions. The end of a race can be a relief, but that does not mean the competition is finished. The cowboys take their stress and anger back to the barns, and resorting to fisticuffs has not been uncommon. Kelly Sutherland recalls one dispute: "The best fight I ever saw was between two sober fifty-five-year-old men, Lloyd Nelson and Bill Greenwood, in the infield at Red Deer, Alberta. After a race, they pulled in. Lloyd was upset, and he hollered at his son to hold the horses. Lloyd then yelled, 'Bill, get off the wagon! Get your son to hold the horses. You and I are going to fight!'"

Sutherland continues, "As these two humongous men faced off, Bill asked, 'What about?' Lloyd replied, 'You've crowded me once too often. You know better and I'm not putting up with it.' The fight began: two men, toe to toe, bare knuckles — smack, smack, smack. They punched one another for about ten minutes.

Finally, Lloyd Nelson won the fight." Sutherland shakes his head, "Here I was, eighteen years old, and I figure if I crowd some guy out, I'm going to get the shit beat right out of me."

Kelly Sutherland is no stranger to hostility in the barns. He says, "When the race is over, harsh words can be shared, especially with guys who you compete with consistently. Guys will say, 'You're too close! Back off!' There are challenges back and forth."

Tempers flare when cowboys feel their horses' safety has been jeopardized. In every race, wagon cowboys have implicit trust in their competitors' skills and competence. Sutherland says, "At any time, our whole existence in the sport is dependent on somebody's whim. When your horses are right next to a wagon, if that driver makes one wrong move, not only do you lose your livestock, but you could get hurt. That's why the emotions run pretty high between individuals; you're in very tight corners all the time. If somebody gets too close, you get mad, 'cause you get scared; you don't know what the hell he's doing." He emphasizes, "I get upset, especially at the older guys. I know what they are doing, and they know what they're doing. Sometimes I get angry, but then I laugh afterwards and think, 'Would I have done that?' Probably."

Another cause for dispute in the barns can arise from the "handshake loyalty" between drivers and their outriders. Tradition asserts that outriders race "first call" for the driver who offered them their first chance to outride. First call is the outrider's priority outfit. Committing to remain with this driver is based on integrity and honour, yet it is tested by the lure of money.

Bensmiller believes the outriders' loyalty should not be open for discussion. He says, "I tried to hire an outrider, and he wanted a hundred dollars per ride" — which is a top-end price for an outrider's seventy-five seconds' worth of work. Bensmiller told him that if he was penalty-free he would pay him the one hundred dollars, but contrary to usual protocol, the outrider wanted the money up front. Bensmiller asked, "Are you going to screw up?" The outrider replied, "No, I ain't screwing up." Buddy said, "Well then, you should stick by your word, and ride before you're paid."

By enticing outriders with higher wages, Kelly Sutherland is partly responsible for this friction. He responds, "I kept driving the price up because my sponsors asked me why I was having some penalty trouble. They asked, 'Why isn't so-and-so outriding for you?' The outriders' allegiance will switch if you pay them enough money, and your penalties will decrease with those guys. I feel driving the pay up is good for the outriders."

Bensmiller is not convinced. "We just hand the outriders a horse, they ride it, they give the horse back, and away they go for a hundred bucks. For an hour's worth of work, some outriders make $800 to $1,000 a night. In Ponoka, the prize money was $40,000, and it costs the drivers $34,000 to pay for outriders. That leaves only $6,000 to be spread out between the drivers, and who has the expenses? It just doesn't make sense to me."

With Jim Nevada, there is no second-guessing: his integrity is not open for discussion. Malicious accusations against his sincerity as an outrider hurt more than any physical injury. He says, "At Morris, Manitoba, a horse threw a wreck on me and I badly broke my ribs — I've still got a bone sticking out. Later I heard people talking behind my back about how I faked it. That pissed me off."

To continue racing, Nevada stoked himself with painkillers. He says, "If they'd shot me in the head with a gun, I would've just smiled. At Strathmore, Hugh Sinclair had a runaway, so I jumped on a horse and pulled his outfit up. Well, I could've lifted a house for the amount of dope I was on."

In time, Nevada's ribs healed. Time also mends rifts between rival cowboys and restores friendships. Nevada relates, "Driving in the Dash for Cash at Edmonton, I used a borrowed horse in my outfit, and I wiped out three of Neal Walgenbach's outriders. Neal and I are pretty good friends, and I felt like shit. They fined the crap outta me, but good friends always make up. A few weeks later, Neal invited us over for a barbecue — that's the kind of guy he is."

Mistrust among competitors can take on a more serious tone, however, particularly when a fellow competitor is suspected of having pulled a ruse. In 1995, veteran driver Ward Willard won the Calgary Stampede by a literal horse's nose, coming from behind to beat Buddy Bensmiller. Bensmiller thought he himself had the race won. "Willard's wagon was behind me, but his one lead horse was just ahead of the other one and popped the clicker first." Willard won by three-hundredths of a second. After the race, the horses were drug tested. (In an age when drug use has become so prevalent in sports, drug testing has come to be recognized as necessary, so even chuckwagon athletes are tested — both the two-legged and the four-legged varieties.)

Bensmiller notes that before the test results were back, "Ward stopped in three times to the race office looking for his $50,000 cheque. He kept stopping, wanting his money. Finally the officials said, 'Shit, give him the money if he's so sure he's got it.'" The test results then came back positive. Willard's horse was found to have traces of the banned substance procaine. Procaine is a fast-acting local anaesthetic that is mixed with penicillin and used to soothe the sting of infections. It is also suspected to have the capability of masking other substances, although Dr. Larry Watrin, chief veterinarian for the Alberta Racing Commision, denied that procaine can act as a masking agent, and further stated that it does not have any stimulating effect and is not a performance-enhancing drug. Nevertheless, in light of the discovery, Willard was fined $1,000, but was allowed to keep the balance of the $50,000 cheque.

Bensmiller, Tom Glass, and Kelly Sutherland, the three other competitors in the final heat, all felt Willard should have been stripped of the title. Willard was unfazed and unwilling to return his cheque. To show his confidence publicly, Willard called a press conference and challenged each of the three finalists to a tournament. Willard's calculated tournament would have consisted of a separate race against each of them, ensuring they could not collaborate to block him on the track. All of his rivals declined, but the sport revealed its participants' human frailties.

Bensmiller elected not to fight further. He explains his decision: "If I go after the fifty thousand dollars, I look like an idiot. I don't want to drag my sponsor through the shit and the mud. I don't believe in bad publicity, and I don't want any of it. I've worked too damn hard to get the name I've got to be in a pissin' match with them guys." Bensmiller believes his approach has paid off. He is still supported solidly by sponsors and has rightly retained his earned image as a gallant sportsman and honourable cowboy.

Although reluctant to joust in the court of public relations, Bensmiller does not hesitate to challenge his nemesis and colleague Kelly Sutherland. Bensmiller proposes there may be more than luck or skill to Sutherland's frequent success. Buddy offers this example from one Calgary Stampede competition: "In 1998, after considerable rain, [the Stampede maintenance staff] rebuilt the track on two different days. The first day they rebuilt the 3 and 4 barrels, the next night 1 and 2. Calgary [Stampede officials] couldn't understand why they did it, other than Kelly told them to. Kelly was with the equipment when the work was done."

Muddy track conditions can critically hinder the horses and wagons, especially in the barrel turns. Buddy continues, "So I asked the guy in Calgary, 'You explain to me how you can build these two barrels up one night, and then these two barrels up, and tell me its fair. He said, 'By geez, we've done the wrong thing.' I said, 'You can bet you've done the wrong thing. Why did you do it?'

"I had a shot to win it too, but I ended up on the goddam Barrel 1 when Kelly was on Barrel 3, and on Barrel 2 when he was on Barrel 4. The next night he was on Barrel 1 and the infield was rebuilt. Calgary agreed they screwed up." Bensmiller laughs, "They told me to keep an eye on the track, so I rode out at 6:30 a.m., to check it. The first guy I met standing in the infield with the trucks was Kelly."

Bensmiller and Sutherland have a colourful history discussing track conditions. For many years, Sutherland has been a "track man," responsible for ensuring the quality and safety of the tour racetracks. Bensmiller relates, "It was raining the first night I raced at Grande Prairie. Kelly was on Barrel 4, so he left the track alone. The next night Kelly was on Barrel 1. That afternoon, I was shoeing horses and somebody told me there was a grader working on the track. I said, 'Bullshit there is!' The show had already started, and the track can't be touched."

Bensmiller went out on the track. He recalls, "I asked Kelly, 'What the hell are you doing?' 'Well, what do you think?' Kelly said. 'I'm getting the track packed for me tonight.' I said, 'You can't do that, you rotten son of a bitch.' I just ripped a strip off of him. He said, 'It's not safe to run on,' and I replied, 'You made us run on it last night, and now you're telling me you can't run on it?'"

After this incident, the rest of the World Professional Chuckwagon Association drivers also appointed Bensmiller as a "track man," to work alongside Sutherland. Even though the horses' health and the races' safety rely upon a well-built track, the job is a thankless one. Buddy says, "Every time I do something, the drivers feel I'm doing it for myself, but it's the sport you've got to think for. I've always said drivers are worse than kindergarten kids; you can't talk reason to half of them, and every time you do something for the sport, they say you're doing it for yourself. You can't even send them home to their mother."

Bensmiller and Sutherland maintain a competitive friendship. Bensmiller says, "Most of the drivers won't stand up to Kelly. I don't have a problem with it. I think Kelly kind of respects me, too, because of it. I don't get a lot of respect from the son of a bitch, but he does pay attention."

Chuckwagon competition also takes place in boardrooms and meeting halls. In 1979, a dispute between the Canadian Professional Rodeo Association (CPRA), which included the pro chuckwagon drivers, and the Calgary Stampede resulted in Calgary shutting out Kelly Sutherland and the existing drivers. Sutherland says, "At that time, there was no financial benefit to be a chuckwagon driver. None. We wanted a huge increase in prize money, which was wrong, and we wanted it all in one year. We were requesting twenty-five percent of the gate, which was about one million dollars. When push came to shove, the Stampede said they would meet the increase, but they couldn't do it in one year." Kelly reflects, "I think we were naïve."

With the pro wagon cowboys refusing to race at Calgary, the Stampede sought out and welcomed alternative wagon cowboys from northern Alberta. Sutherland grimaces, "The wagons that the Stampede found took a reduction in prize money. They set the sport back ten years. That to me was a disgrace to wagon racing." The incoming drivers included the young Buddy Bensmiller, who went on to win the Rangeland Derby that year.

To compete against the Stampede, and to attract wagon fans, Sutherland and the pro drivers raced instead at the Battle of the Giants, in High River, south of Calgary. To strengthen their political voice, the drivers left the CPRA and formed the World Professional Chuckwagon Association.

During this period, Kelly and his father bought the Claremont Hotel, outside of Grande Prairie. They renamed it the Sutherland Inn, and Kelly turned his attention to developing a lavish nightclub. Although he continued to race, his focus moved away from horses to the family's business.

After three years of arguing, the WPCA drivers returned to Calgary in 1982, but Sutherland was not invited. Sutherland says, "When we returned to Calgary, the Stampede board held me responsible for a lot of our association's political actions. The Stampede felt that if I had not been so adamant initially, the drivers may not have left. I always seemed to be at loggerheads with the Stampede board, but I was trying to make the sport better for them and for us. I had tried to improve facilities for our people and our horses, and I tried to rectify rules that weren't fair to everybody. They told me I had become a pain in the ass, but I always put the sport first."

Ralph Klein, who was then mayor of Calgary, was instrumental in helping the blackballed Sutherland. Kelly says, "To me, Ralph is the 'keeper of the average guy,' and that is why he is so popular. He'd read what was going on in the paper. He felt I was unjustly done by, and he called me to his office." Through Klein, the Stampede invited Sutherland to race.

Looking back, Sutherland says, "I never did like the animosity or the fighting, because it became personal to me. I was fighting for the sport, and I'll always fight for the sport. Then or now, there's no way we shouldn't be making a bunch of money in this sport. People risk their lives." He adds, "I do know, it probably turned out better for the sport. Our actions proved to Calgary the value of the WPCA members."

Two years later, when Sutherland competed at the 1984 Stampede, he felt there were still ill feelings, and he believed the judges were squaring up some issues. "I got a very cheap penalty," describes Sutherland. "I told my sponsor, The Calgary Herald, I was done if the judging was going to be like that. They said that was fine. I left midway in the Stampede and spent a couple of weeks fishing in Kelowna, British Columbia. I said I was shutting down. I'd won Calgary enough times."

Sutherland sat out the entire 1985 season. During his sabbatical, he realized he could not expect any advantages if he did not put his full effort into the sport. He affirms, "My competitors demonstrated hard work can outplay talent. Lots of people work a hell of a lot harder than somebody who has talent, and they end up winning." Sutherland doggedly picked up the wagon lines, aggressively pushing himself back into the sport. In 1986, he made his triumphant return, again winning the Calgary Stampede.

As described, Sutherland's journey to prominence has been marked by controversy. For over half of his career, he has been embroiled in some sort of contention, whether with race committees or with competitors. The King has not enjoyed a peaceful reign. Yet he states, "I kind of thrived on it. It didn't bother me one bit."

Due to these battles, Kelly has acquired the public persona of being hostile and combative. He is the only driver to be boisterously heckled by spectators. "At the races, I get as many boos as cheers," says Kelly, "but I always maintained, as long as it is a fan, it is good for wagon racing. People boo the hell out of me, but they are either Dorchester or Glass fans. They may hate me or like me, but those people are prepared to pay to watch us and follow the sport."

Sutherland clarifies, "People say they 'hate' NHL player Theoren Fleury. How can they hate somebody they don't even know? But whoever says that is watching hockey, and they know where Fleury is in the scoring race, and that's good for the sport. Pro athletes need to understand that.

"What I found is that when you first win and you're a rising star, people love you. Your competitors, your fans, everybody loves you. If you win a few times, that's just about enough — they still kind of like you. When you win as much as I do, my competitors and even my best friends say, 'Look, you've won enough — now quit.' I don't blame them, I'd think the same way."

To win, and to win often, the cowboys need luck on their side. Sutherland, Bensmiller, and Nevada all court Lady Luck. Every cowboy is on her dance card, and they all have two-stepped with her. The cowboys know her affections, and her rebukes. But even when a cowboy offers his most heartfelt advances, she is not necessarily swayed his way. Her fickleness both beguiles and distresses the cowboys. They estimate that forty to seventy percent of their success is tied to her charms, but they can never predict when she will ride with them, nor how long she will stay.

Good luck is an indispensable blessing; bad luck is an unwanted curse. Buddy Bensmiller describes, "I used to tie my good horses in the barn and use them very little [while] waiting for Calgary, but I'd get there and an outrider would knock a barrel and cost me anyway. Or I used the horses at earlier shows, and a driver would nail a horse. For four years I've had somebody come narrow, hit my horses, and I haven't had my good outfit by the time I get to Calgary."

Bensmiller also knows how quickly good luck can disappear. At the 1992 Calgary Stampede, Buddy was leading after eight days of racing. On the ninth day, he was hooked against Tom Glass, Kelly Sutherland, and Dallas Dorchester. He describes the start of that race: "It was all mud. Tommy pulled his outfit in ahead of the barrel, so we waited and waited for him to set back. Then Kelly's team jumped ahead. Just as Kelly got his horses back in place, my horses went into the air, and they blew the horn."

The lead horses knocked Buddy's outrider down. The outrider missed both barrels and did not finish the race. Buddy was assessed nine seconds in penalties and missed the final heat by two-hundredths of a second. He laments, "I won six out of ten day moneys [prize money awarded to the outfit with the fastest time for that evening's races] that year, so that shows how quickly it can go out the back door." Bensmiller adds, "I've never had an outfit like that one. After injuries in the winter, by the next year I only had one out of the four horses left. That's how fast a great outfit can be gone. I've always had bad luck that way."

Drivers must also recognize when Lady Luck has given an outrider the cold shoulder. Kelly Sutherland has seen it happen. He says, "In 1999, I fired an outrider. I did not want to do it because it is really devastating for an individual, but the fact of the matter is anybody can get on a cold streak. It's like a goalie that can't stop a puck. You've got to get him out of there for his own benefit." Kelly recalls the outrider's reaction. "My guy blew up, and I said, 'Sorry, maybe I'll hire you again later.' When I'm winning and on top, there is tremendous pressure on those individuals, and I'm not doing them a bit of good by allowing them to stay in there."

To woo good fortune, the cowboys adopt superstitious practices. Jim Nevada always wears the same shirt for races. He says, "I had a Washington Redskins shirt when I just outrode. People tried to steal it, and once it was held for ransom. That shirt wore out, and now I own a Denver Broncos championship shirt. The first year I wore it, I set a Calgary track record and won day money. I don't go anywhere without wearing my Broncos T-shirt. In the winter, I hide it in the house."

Kelly Sutherland has also followed some interesting rituals. He recalls how he used to try to ensure his luck would not wash away: "The first few years in Calgary I didn't have a full-fledged shower, I used to have a sponge bath. I recall that as a very strange quirk. I shower regularly now."

Counter to cowboy fashion, Kelly also developed the habit of wearing running shoes when he races. But it is a practical habit. As he drives, Sutherland shifts across the wagon seat constantly, using his feet for balance and leverage. He says, "Ever since I outrode, I've worn light rubber-soled shoes, and I bind them really, really tight, so they basically cut the circulation off on my feet. I don't feel very protected unless they are done up tight. After I'm done racing, it'll strike me that my feet are hurting, and I'll undo my shoes."

Partly out of superstition and partly from the comfort offered by sticking to a pattern, drivers will also follow specific practices when hooking their horses for a race. The horses are harnessed in a certain order. Some cowboys do it themselves; other drivers just jump into the seat and let their assistants hook their horses. Sutherland offers why a routine helps the drivers: "When they are hooking, drivers don't like a lot of people around. They're focused, and getting themselves mentally prepared. They don't want to talk to people."

When you are perched on the King's throne, the fall from grace can be particularly steep. Kelly Sutherland knows the anguish that superstar athletes face when they go through those periods when they know how to win, they are expected to win, but they cannot win.

Sutherland describes, "Three times in about five years, my outfit hit a barrel [while] going for the fifty thousand dollars at Calgary. The first time, I had won the race, but an outrider knocked the barrel. I had the money and the pickup truck won, plus the bonuses from my sponsor and the bronze trophies."

Following the race, Sutherland drove into the barns and found the guilty outrider crying, obviously extremely upset. Kelly distanced himself. He says, "I was livid. I'm that type of competitive individual. If I, or one of the crew, mess up big time, for a big amount of money, I've just got to get away. I will go away by myself into a stall somewhere, and just spend some time there."

Sutherland returned from his retreat, and the outrider was still weeping. Sutherland grabbed him and shook him. Kelly recalls what happened next: "I asked him, 'Look, what's going on? Nobody died did they? I didn't see anybody die.' The outrider said, 'I cost you all that money.' I said, 'Forget about it. It's history, we ain't standing the son of a bitch up. Next year, don't make the mistake again. There's nobody more pissed off than I am, but forget about it — it's done. Let's go drink the champ's whiskey.'"

In the Stampede finals the next two years, Sutherland hit the barrels himself. Each barrel knocked down was a minimum financial loss of $100,000 in prize money and sponsorship. Kelly says, "The first time was my mistake: I went right over top of the barrel. The lead team ducked, and I let them duck. The second final, the left-wheeler slipped when he started. He couldn't catch up, and the wagon's back wheel caught the barrel. After the last time, I just went and sat by myself in the barn and cussed myself for so long. I didn't sleep very well for a week."

Sutherland adds, "After I hit it two years in a row, I said to myself, 'If I ever draw again in the finals, I don't care if I take an hour to get around, I won't hit another barrel.' And I haven't."

Hitting those barrels taxed Sutherland's mental reserve. He describes, "When I had trouble and I hit those barrels, I'm not scared to say some nights I just literally cried by myself, or drove away in a pickup alone. I was just so emotional. For me there's no second place, and to me that just proved I wasn't that great." He chastises himself, "I get every advantage, I draw Barrel 1, which is the barrel I need to win, and what do I do? I drive overtop the son of a bitch. Firstly, I disappoint my sponsor; secondly, my family; and thirdly, reassure to all the drivers that I ain't that good, which is totally against what I'm trying to prove." Sutherland also admits, "Quite frankly, after that is when I started consuming alcohol pretty heavy, too. I started drinking heavier and heavier."

Kelly considered himself fortunate just to get three shots at the Calgary finals, nevertheless. He says, "Lots of people never make the finals! I hear guys crying about hitting a barrel and how much day money it cost them. I start laughing, and tell them, 'I hit three barrels for fifty thousand dollars apiece — don't cry. You'll get no sympathy from me, boys. Just try that and see how well you sleep for a week.'"

The self-induced pressure to win is constant with Sutherland, but every driver feels the psychological threat of the long barrel — Barrel 1. Although Barrel 1 offers the best opportunity for an outfit to gain the strategic rail position, the cowboy must not be out-turned by any other wagon. If another driver turns his bottom barrel first and takes the rail position, the Barrel 1 wagon will have little chance to overcome the leader. It will become trapped by wagons to the front and side.

Therefore, the cowboy on Barrel 1 wagon has to charge to the top barrel turn. Sutherland describes, "When you're going for broke, especially for the fifty thousand dollars, you're thinking, 'This is too much time, too much time. I've got to turn. I gotta turn!'"

Which cowboy gets which barrel position in the Stampede's final heat is determined by a draw. Prior to the race, the four cowboys who have made it into the finals draw coloured billiard balls out of a box. In 1998, Sutherland was again in the finals. Sizing up his team of horses, he knew he needed his dreaded Barrel 1 — the grief barrel — to win. He drew Barrel 1.

Kelly says, "Everybody who knew me close, including my family and competitors, thought I was going to hit the son of a bitch, guaranteed." He laughs, "For once there were cheers in the stands when I drew number one." The fans who were rooting against Sutherland felt he was going to hit a barrel again.

As he hooked his horses, Kelly promised himself, "This is one time I'm going to reach really down deep, and I'm going to find what wagon racing is all about to me. If those horses work, that's the barrel I need to win it."

He revels, "When I did turn that son of a bitch, I couldn't believe it that I actually made it. Once I drew Barrel 1 again in 1999, I had so much confidence. The last series of wins in the 1990s were very important for me mentally — a regeneration. They added ten years onto my wagon racing life."

Buddy Bensmiller surmises Kelly's fortune in drawing Barrel 1 in '98 and '99 had to do more with good vision than good luck. Bensmiller says, "Before we draw the billiard balls out of the box, they take the lid off, hold the box at waist height, shake it, lift it above our heads, and then we draw. When we are reaching up, there's no way the balls change places when they shake the box."

Buddy continues, "As the first guy to draw, Kelly knew exactly where the number one ball was; I know for a fact because I saw all the colours myself. I told the Stampede, 'The balls just roll up and down the box; odds ain't good they're switching spots. How many years has he drawn Barrel 1? You must think he's a lucky son of a bitch.'"

Knowing how frustrating bad luck is, Sutherland relishes any lingering pattern of good luck. He argues, "When you win the Stampede as many times as I have, goddam it, there's no doubt you've got to have a lot of luck. In 1999, my outrider came around and tapped the bottom barrel. It just wavered." Kelly chuckles, "The other drivers' sponsors were standing there blowing. They don't hate me, but they were hoping the barrel fell. The next time he ticks the barrel, shit, it might go down."

Sutherland's Stampede winning streak ended in 2000. Kelly actually won the race, but he was assessed a one-second penalty for being out-of-lane exiting from the barrel turns on Barrel 1. In a dramatic climax, driver Hugh Sinclair won his first Calgary Stampede.

Competition occurs on many planes in wagon racing. The game is played on the emotional, physical, and mental levels — with a good dose of chance thrown in. Some cowboys will broadcast their drive through braggadocio, while others will mask it in hardened silence. All attempt to conceal the stress and strains of the sport beneath their leather hides. As each cowboy searches for a winning advantage, he also recognizes his need for luck. But luck will take the cowboys only so far. Preparation, focus, and most importantly, the hunger to win are what earn championships.

CHAPTER 6

Vindicating Victories

Driver Rick Fraser was trying to make the cut for the Calgary Stampede, but he was getting too many penalties. He needed an outrider. I outrode for him, and he made Calgary by three points. Afterwards, I told him, 'I quit.' He had a big tear in his eye, saying, 'Thanks.' Those are the good memories — when you can help someone out.

JIM NEVADA

The cowboys often taste frustration as they find themselves eating their competitors' dust. But there are also morsels of victory to savour. These accomplishments justify the cowboys' efforts, and they can be as humble as the gratification of bringing a horse back to health, or as prodigious as the triumph of winning the

Calgary Stampede. What brings satisfaction to each cowboy is as varied as the styles of cowboy hats.

Amongst the cowboys' aspirations, the championship buckles still rank at the top. The titles, trophies, and cheques are standards against which peers, sponsors, and fans can gauge the cowboys' skills. Success in the arena launches the cowboys into the status of western heroes. Amidst the awards up for the taking, the Calgary Stampede Rangeland Derby prevails as the ultimate prize.

But the Stampede is also the toughest of prize adjudicators. To earn its glories, most cowboys climb a ladder of achievements. Kelly Sutherland relates, "You come to realize there are different stages for a wagon driver. First, all I wanted to do was win one show, and I did that my first year. Then each year, I managed to win one show, and place in the top ten. Then my goal was to achieve a major win like Calgary."

One of Sutherland's most gratifying moments came early in his career, when he actually lost the Calgary Stampede. In 1972, he raced in the Stampede's final heat against his veteran travelling partner, Ralph Vigen. Vigen was Kelly's role model and confidante, and although Vigen had been a runner-up in eight previous Stampede finals, he had never won.

Sutherland recalls the evening, "I out-turned and outran Ralph, but I had a late outrider. I was runner-up by thirty-six hundredths of a second. Vigen won the race, but he was quite upset. He just hated to get outrun, and I knew that. While we walked back to pick up our buckles, I put my arm around him and said, 'Jesus Christ, smile, you're the champion of Calgary.' He said, 'I never won it. You lost the goddam thing.' I laughed and asked him, 'How many times did you lose it because an outrider was late?'"

Sutherland was just twenty years old at the time. It took him only another two years before he joined Vigen as a Calgary champion. Sutherland recollects his 1974 success, "I couldn't believe I'd won Calgary. It was the highlight of my career. On that day, I never ever believed I could have achieved something like that. I was just the happiest kid in the world."

Sutherland's Stampede win was not a happenstance. That year, Calgary had built a new racetrack, lengthening the race from half a mile to five-eighths of a mile. In preparation, Sutherland had bought distance horses, thoroughbreds who excelled at an extended race.

After Sutherland's win in 1974, he and Ralph Vigen took command of wagon racing for about five years. Sutherland won the Stampede again in '75, '77, and '78, and the Canadian Professional Rodeo Association championship in '77 and '79. Vigen won Calgary in '76, and the CPRA championship in '75, '76, and '79. Kelly says, "It was just like going to a Sunday school picnic, it was no big deal, it was just the way it was."

For the King, his seventy-five-plus chuckwagon championships have not lessened his desire to win. Sutherland's intensity continues to set him apart from his rivals. Even when he is merely reminiscing or describing a race, his face tightens and his fists clench with combative power and urgency. He states, "I love the feeling when I can go out and outrun all the guys, and they have to look at me and realize I've won. But that does not mean when somebody else wins I don't go over and congratulate them. When I first won the Calgary Stampede, all the guys who had won before came over and shook my hand, and that meant so much to me. I never forgot it. So every time somebody else wins, or a young guy wins their first day money, I go over and shake their hand. That's what makes a driver tough, is when they gain that confidence."

Buddy Bensmiller advocates that there is more to success in chuckwagons than simply hoisting a championship bronze trophy. Bensmiller finds his fulfilment in moulding a hard-barrelling team of horses. He says, "I never get too excited about winning. I like to win, I go there to win, but if I don't, I'll be back next year. I get a thrill when you can get an outfit that's popping, really starting and working together like clockwork."

Rather than winning for winning's sake, Bensmiller also recognizes his responsibility to the companies supporting his horses and his family. Always the cowboy gentleman, he states, "Now with the money the sponsors are putting into it, I always try to do better for them so they get their money's worth."

Each season, Bensmiller starts with the same goals. "I'm going to win Calgary and I'm going to win the World championship. I always shoot for Calgary. And I'll be there, if I have the luck to hold everything together. I've got more depth in terms of horsepower than anybody else, but to win a championship, unless there's a personal tie to it, it's just another race."

Bensmiller remembers his first major victory. "Winning the 1979 Calgary Stampede was, and it wasn't, an early highlight." Throughout the '79 racing season, Bensmiller competed with only six driving horses. Buddy recalls what happened on the sixth night of Stampede racing: "Veteran driver Tommy Dorchester cut me down on the backstretch. He was a little bit ahead of me, and I don't know why, but he just pulled into me and wiped me out, killing three horses on me."

At that time, Bensmiller and Dorchester raced in opposing wagon associations. The distrust and animosity were tangible in the barns. Dorchester came to Bensmiller and offered him horses, but Bensmiller chased him out of his barn. Buddy flatly states, "I didn't want his goddam horses."

Following the accident, Bensmiller borrowed his father's second lead team. Using the loaned horses, he managed to still win the show. But the victory was bittersweet, and after receiving his trophy Bensmiller said, "I wouldn't have raced if I knew what was going to happen. I'm not happy about the whole week, even though I won. It cost me my horses."

One of Buddy's most emotional victories was in honour of his friend Randy Evans, who had been fatally injured outriding at Cheyenne in 1986. During a race, Evans's horse fell, throwing him into the path of an oncoming wagon. Bensmiller says, "When I came back and won Cheyenne in '87, that seemed to be the best year. I wanted to win it so bad for Randy."

Two years later, in 1989, Bensmiller won his second Calgary Stampede. Again, fellowship and camaraderie were woven into his achievement.

In 1989 Bensmiller and his lifelong friend, George Normand, both owned superb outfits, and they were hooked together in the final heat. Bensmiller drew Barrel 2; Normand, Barrel 4; Richard Cosgrave, Barrel 1; and Dallas Dorchester, Barrel 3. Bensmiller recalls, "I barrelled out, and Cosgrave forced me to run two-wagons wide the whole way around. George fell into the rail behind me and took a run at me coming home. All four wagons finished within one second of each other, and I only beat George by six-hundredths of a second. It wasn't much." Buddy adds, "I think that was probably the most exciting race Calgary has ever had for a final. The Calgary Stampede will say it themselves."

George Normand was first off his wagon to shake his friend's hand. A photograph taken shortly after the race shows Normand smiling and congratulating Bensmiller. Bensmiller uses both of his muscular hands to grip Normand's outstretched hand, and a gentleness is evident. Between these two hardened cowboys, a reciprocal respect and fondness shines. Their eyes radiate with common joy — two boyhood friends fulfilling their childhood dreams.

Bensmiller says, "George ended up with the pickup truck [for having the best ten-day aggregate time], and I got the money. He probably figured it should have happened the other way around." Today, the three-foot-square $50,000 cheque remains framed and hanging in the Bensmillers' living room. On the other side of the room hangs a pencil drawing of the cherished photograph. Describing the drawing, Buddy says, "It was a gift from George's wife, who commissioned it. Anybody can blow up a photograph, but the artist did such a good job of it. It's better than a snapshot."

During competition, the cowboys' cool demeanour masks knotted stomachs. Since wagon races are held in the evenings, the cowboys' nerves and imaginations have all day to brew and boil.

With more than fifty tour outriding victories and a record six Calgary Stampede outriding buckles, Jim Nevada appreciates the pre-race tension. He recalls, "The first time I won Calgary, I rode for Dallas Dorchester. There is a lot of pressure on a young rider, and I was pretty nervous. All day long before the race, I thought, 'If I don't get that tent peg in, I will cost Dallas twenty thousand dollars.'"

In the final heat, holding his horse's reins, Nevada marched up to the back of Dallas's wagon. He grabbed and pulled out his tent peg as Dorchester wheeled to a stop. He prepared to throw the peg into the wagon. He describes, "The tent peg weighed fifty pounds instead of three pounds. It seemed like everything was heavier. Now, the finals are just another race."

Each outrider or driver responds differently to the pressure of racing. Nevada is recognized for his pranks and jokes, keeping himself and his crew laughing. Some outriders, however, never learn how to quell their anxieties. Nevada says, "Those guys didn't start long and they didn't last outriding long. After just lighting their cigarette, they'd take one puff and it would go right to the filter. You know damn well they were nervous."

Other outriders pace the hallways, stall-walking through the barns, while some cowboys resort to slapping themselves to try to find peace. Nevada laughs, "Randy Armstrong was a nervous outrider, and before a race he'd be walking around slapping his face. One day Lyle Panbrum came up to him and gave him a knuckle sandwich. Randy just saw stars. Lyle said, 'That should do you for a week.' Lyle was just so sick of seeing that slapping shit."

Nevada adds it is more fun to win as an outrider with specific cowboys. One of Nevada's most memorable outriding victories occurred in 1991, when he was again riding for Dallas Dorchester.

In '91, two days after the start of the Calgary Stampede, Tom Dorchester, Dallas's father and an eminent wagon driver, died. To honour his father, Dallas decided to continue competing at the Stampede. Only hours after the funeral, the cowboys were back racing. Nevada recalls his and his fellow outriders' combined efforts to keep Dallas competitive: "Dallas had a hot-snapping outfit. One night I missed the pegs, so I let go of my horse, reloaded the dragging pegs, and my partner passed me my horse. We made it on time." He continues, "That was the kind of week it was. When things blew up, they blew up. We had to ride like we were possessed. I took every advantage I could to be on time — cutting through holes, making openings. We managed to keep Dallas in there, and won the show."

The feelings brought to the surface by the death of Dallas Dorchester's father illustrate the emotions the cowboys link to their victories and the sport. Families and friends are entwined in the sport's sublime moments. The cowboys' triumphs are a product of the community. Buddy Bensmiller agrees, "For me, wagon racing is for people as far as I'm concerned, and there are always little things you tie into winning."

For Kelly Sutherland, the decade from 1987 to the mid-1990s awarded more kicks than kudos. Despite his sincerest efforts, and even though he regularly made the Calgary finals, Sutherland could not win. Eventually, the amassed losses became debilitating for a competitor so driven to succeed.

Sutherland was in a bad-luck wreck that kept replaying itself. For example, in 1996, Sutherland was primed to race in the Calgary final. His horses and his self-assurance finally seemed to have rebounded. Late during the Stampede week, he took his horses out for their morning exercise. On horseback, he led them down the Calgary backstretch. One horse got loose and as Sutherland dismounted to control the problem, the four horses panicked and trampled over him. They ran four abreast through an open gate, slipped on the asphalt, and fell, all sprawling across the pavement.

Kelly describes, "The horses slid under the parked trailers. One banged his head so hard his eyes were swollen shut. Another had a hole knocked in his skull. The others were shaken up but not seriously hurt." To carry on in the races, Sutherland borrowed horses from a colleague, Hugh Sinclair. He still made the finals, but lost to Edgar Baptiste. The trials of the sport were exhausting Sutherland, and he was unsure of how much he had left to give to the sport.

Twelve months later, the blinders of defeat were finally lifted. Kelly states, "Against all odds, I came off of Barrel 4, and won the Stampede against Buddy Bensmiller, Jason [Glass], and Tommy Glass — the three toughest there." Although it was his sixth Stampede victory, this particular win rejuvenated him — he was as emotional as the first time he won the Stampede.

In achieving this win, Sutherland had raced from the Barrel 4 position. In all four years prior to 1997, Kelly had also drawn the disadvantaged Barrel 3 or 4 for the Stampede finals. Although Barrel 4 has the shortest distance between top and bottom barrels, the wagon must travel the farthest to reach the rail position. Thus the three wagons ahead of Barrel 4 all have the advantage in gaining the rail. Similarly, the wagon on Barrel 3 is disadvantaged against the wagons on Barrels 1 and 2.

Describing the process of drawing for barrel position, Sutherland notes, "When I pick the balls out of the box, I always grab a number, then I drop the son of a bitch and pick up another. In '97, I was picking third and there were two numbers left in the hat: Barrel 4 and Barrel 1. I again picked Barrel 4." Sutherland winces as he recalls the moment. "I got back to the barns and I told my son, Mark, 'How dumb I am. I had Barrel 1 in my hand and I figured, "No way, it's got to be Barrel 4," so I threw it back.' I felt terrible, terrible."

Sutherland adds, "When I drew Barrel 4, those other drivers were just relieved, especially Tommy. So, I said to myself, 'This is it!' I then told Mark, 'I'll tell you, if those sons of bitches win this one, they are going to be rattling, don't think they ain't.'"

That evening, Sutherland stoked up his confidence. He says, "I seized the advantage in '97. I made an effort to come mentally prepared before the race because my horses had to be prepared too." He conveyed his conviction and fighting spirit to his horses. (Any dog owner who has ever been in a foul mood and watched the family dog slink away or hunker down knows that animals pick up their master's mood.) Kelly says, "I warmed the horses up far more than usual and they understood this was different. The hotter they got, the more they wanted to work. I just figured, 'You boys gotta figure this out, she's go for broke.'"

Sutherland was gambling in warming up his horses to such a fever pitch. Since he had drawn Barrel 4, he had to drive his wagon to the starting barrel first, and then wait for the other drivers to pull in. If any other driver had problems, forcing him to linger too long, Sutherland's horses would jump ahead. "I'd be left dead in the water," he says. "As soon as the horses jump ahead and you're in a storm, you're going to be out-turned, so there's a huge gamble. I could tell the horses were ready, they were going to move. I told my outriders, 'You guys get ready, we are leaving quick!'"

Sutherland describes the race, "When the horn went, those horses literally exploded. We were turning in just a split second. My stove man threw the stove ten feet, and it just landed in the box as I turned. I glanced over in the infield and knew it was over for them boys [Sutherland's competitors]. I was going by as their wagons were turning down. I got to the front end, and shit, I was almost two lengths in front. It was an unbelievable feeling."

Mark rounds the third corner at Lethbridge, Alberta, on June 19, 1999.
(CAROL AND PAUL EASTON, WAGON PHOTOGRAPHY)

3

PREVIOUS SPREAD: Mark turns the bottom barrel and hits the track at Strathmore, Alberta, July 31, 1996. (CAROL AND PAUL EASTON, WAGON PHOTOGRAPHY)

Mark comes down the homestretch at the Calgary Stampede Rangeland Derby on July 11, 1996. (CAROL AND PAUL EASTON, WAGON PHOTOGRAPHY)

Covered in mud, Mark is seen waving to the crowd at the Ponoka Stampede in 1998, accompanied by Al Barr. (SUTHERLAND FAMILY COLLECTION)

FACING PAGE: Mark races down the backstretch at Trochu, Alberta, May 20, 1996. (CAROL AND PAUL EASTON, WAGON PHOTOGRAPHY)

Troy turns the top barrel at Klondike Days, Edmonton, Alberta, July 1999.
(CAROL AND PAUL EASTON, WAGON PHOTOGRAPHY)

Troy charges for home at the Calgary Stampede, July 10, 1999.
(CAROL AND PAUL EASTON, WAGON PHOTOGRAPHY)

Wearing his grandfather's cowboy hat, Troy fights off a challenger in Lethbridge, Alberta, June 19, 1999. (CAROL AND PAUL EASTON, WAGON PHOTOGRAPHY)

Sutherland now needed to check on his outriders. "If the crew had done their job, it was over. I looked behind and the pegs were loaded. By the time I turned for home, an outrider rode up beside me and gave me the nod."

Sutherland was still keeping an eye on the other wagons to see if they were catching up to him. He says, "When you turn for home, you've got to watch that you're not gathered up by the wire. Those horses can only run so fast, for so long. They either burn it up at the front end or coming home. Once I got closer to the wire, it was one of the few times I was standing right up in the wagon. It was one of the most emotional highs I've ever been on."

He adds, "After the race there was the emotional time of waiting for the judges, but you know you've beaten most of the guys because they [have driven] back to the barns. They left me sitting there. They usually know better than anyone, and if there's a chance, the drivers stay on the track." Finally, Joe Carbury announced the King had won.

This victory was a turning point in Kelly Sutherland's career. It refocused and refreshed his enthusiasm for the sport, leading to his subsequent Stampede victories in '98 and '99.

Jim Nevada earned some of his cowboy toughness in 1999, when he won his first WPCA tour show at Lethbridge, Alberta. Nevada admits that every other driver of his generation had already won a tour show. He says, "I started to think, 'Holy cripe, I am a loser.' I didn't want to be remembered as a guy who was a good competitor but hadn't won squat."

As Nevada prepared for the final race in Lethbridge, his confidence was soaring. He recalls, "My outriding crew was as nervous as hell, but I wasn't going to lose it. It was my show to win. It was my turn, and piss on everyone else. I went out there as aggressive as ever, and we won."

This victory launched Nevada into the '99 Calgary Stampede with a new boldness, and for the first time, he earned a spot in the $50,000 final. Regrettably, in order to stay competitive over all ten days, he had exhausted his horses. Nevada explains, "I ran the final race with only one horse I owned. The horses that had got me there, they were done. I wasn't going to blast them again just to finish last in the race. It's like when you're coaching a team, you know which player has a little left in them, and in my barn there was nothing left." Nevada finished fourth in the race.

Nevada adds, "After Calgary, I could've slept for about a month. I was mentally drained, but then we had to go to Edmonton. I left all the good horses at home, so they could eat grass, oats, and take 'er easy. I wish I could've too."

Nevertheless, Nevada knows Lethbridge and Calgary were significant in his career development. He states, "In '99, I went through 'the wall.' I now know I can compete with the Kellys and Buddys, and I can outrun them. It's taken me longer than most drivers, but I started further down the steps than most."

To uphold their competitive edge, the drivers never cease to educate themselves. Buddy Bensmiller remarks, "I learn every day, and I keep racing because there is more I can learn. If you quit learning, you quit living. Especially here where you're working with horses."

He adds, "There's nothing better than being on top to learn. When you're on top, everyone shoots for you. Once you're there you know you can get there again; it gives you more drive to be there again. When you win, it makes you tougher. The guys who have driven for twenty years and never won anything, I don't know what brings them back."

To stay a barrel ahead, Buddy is constantly planning how he can adapt or change horses to achieve his goals. He says, "When the Calgary Stampede is over, the first thing I talk about Monday morning is what I'm going to do for next year — how I'm going to change things."

Bensmiller is respected for placing a higher priority on how he wins, rather than how often. Bensmiller shares, "Lots of guys will do anything to win, but that's not the way I am. It's the same with the boys I coach hockey: we go every weekend to win, but we'll win 'er fair and square.

"With many drivers, if they ran fifteenth and I was seventeenth, the first thing to come out of their mouths was 'I outran Buddy Bensmiller' — even if I hit a barrel or had a bad run. To me, I never went out there to outrun anybody, I went there to outrun everybody. I've always been that way. I don't give a shit if that guy outran me today or yesterday, I race to win the day moneys, or as close as I can. I think that attitude's a downfall of a lot of guys — they're shooting their sights for one guy. To me, one guy is the same as another."

Bensmiller believes, "I have a level of confidence other drivers don't. It's been a bonus. I'm not saying I can't do anything wrong: I make mistakes, there's no doubt about it. I don't want to look bad in front of somebody, so I try harder at it and work harder at it. I am willing to hook three or four outfits in snowstorms when no one else is working their horses, and I drive more horses in a year than most guys ever will in a lifetime."

Bensmiller laughs and adds, "Kelly tells everybody I just sit around and work with horses, but I've got one hundred fifty things started, and none finished. I have probably the messiest yard in Alberta; but I'm never home in the summer, I'm buying horses in the fall, and I've got chores and hockey in the winter. People don't realize I haul feed and raise cattle, too. I probably rotate $350,000 per year with my cattle, horses, and wagons. There's a big cost to do it, and if you ain't honest dealing horses, you aren't going to last long in it." Buddy emphasizes, "There are dark hours I put in."

Jim Nevada believes the emotions and stresses found in wagon racing are similar to those in most sports. He says, "It's a typical sport: while you're winning you're on top of the world, but when you can't do squat, you try to figure out what you can change. You don't want to talk to people. It's a coaching situation, and you're trying to figure out how to put your players [horses] together to get the best result. I withdraw from everybody to figure it out. I just sit there and think."

No matter how much money lies on the prize table, Jim Nevada enters each heat, each race, to win. To him, there is no difference between Calgary and any other show. A race is a race. Nevada is competitive and aggressive, and he hates to lose. He details, "I always liked being in the front. I'd rather win my heat than finish third and still win third day money. If you win your race, there's at least two or three other guys you don't have to beat."

Nevada adds, "When you're at the top, it's exciting, especially when you've got an outfit that's starting and turning. There's not a better feeling." On the other hand, says Nevada, "if you're behind, it sucks. When your horses aren't working, you can't outrun a fricken wheelbarrow, and you're out there just to fill races — it's boring, annoying, and not fun. People don't realize how much power there is, but like any sport, when it's not working, it's not fun."

For Kelly Sutherland, his insuperable drive to win was forged by his early experiences. "The first time outriding at the Calgary Stampede," he says, "I was mesmerized. Working for Dave Lewis, I soon realized how great it was just to win day money, and how painful it was for him to lose. Even winning day money, the sponsors and the wives were excited. When something went wrong, I saw how devastated they were."

He adds, "Nobody ever remembers the guy who ran second. Never. I learned that early. The 'what if's,' the 'second place's,' the 'if only's' — they don't work, you've got to be 'number one.' I laid awake at night, trying to figure out horse combinations and how to beat my competitors. Other people who won a lot must have done the same thing, otherwise they wouldn't have won so much.

"I was compelled to prove something to the world, and I don't know where that came from. Whatever I did, I did it to the best of my ability, and if it was wagon racing, there was no second place. I had to go as far as I could. I was just very fortunate, or blessed, to be able to win at it. I'm not sure what I'd ever have done if I couldn't have accomplished it. I'm sure I would've lost interest and done something else."

These defiant cowboys are not governed solely by belligerent testosterone. Underneath their manure-sprayed, rain-soaked, and rough exteriors, strong sentiments exist. And the joy they find in wagon racing is not limited to trophies and buckles. Some of their most meaningful experiences come from helping a friend or being honoured by their peers.

For Jim Nevada, 1999 was an auspicious and pivotal year. Not only did Nevada win his first tour show at Lethbridge, but he was also awarded the Calgary Stampede's Guy Weadick Memorial Award and named the WPCA's Chuckwagon Person of the Year. Both of these awards are judged on the cowboy's contributions to the sport.

The Guy Weadick Memorial Award is perhaps the most respected trophy presented at the Calgary Stampede. Decided through voting by Stampede volunteers, it is given to the rodeo or chuckwagon contestant who best combines outstanding accomplishments with personality, sportsmanship, and how he or she represents the sport. The contestants recognize it as the most esteemed award that they can receive as a cowboy. Orville Strandquist, Richard Cosgrave, and Buddy Bensmiller are the only other wagon drivers to have received the award.

Throughout the 1999 Stampede, Nevada spoke unrepentantly before the media about the lifestyle of the chuckwagon cowboys, and about the concern they have for and care they put into their horses. During the tournament, Nevada also continued to help manage his barn as well as drive all week for injured wagon driver Ron David.

Nevada says, "I do a lot of stuff to promote the sport, but it's not to win awards. I always hated them awards." He adds, "Every award I had been in before had been a favouritism award. It was always 'who knew who.' I didn't understand the Guy Weadick. I didn't realize it is awarded by people who know about the sport. I respect that."

Nevada's forthrightness and sincerity were later singled out in 1999, when he was named the WPCA's Chuckwagon Person of the Year. The commendation came at a time when he was still doubting his efforts. He says, "Some of the older drivers said I still had years before I would win that award."

Nevada is known for his direct, no-nonsense approach. "I'm not the shiniest guy around," he says. "Whenever people talk about me in a meeting, they say, 'Nevada lacks the chrome.' At meetings people don't have to figure me out; I put all the cards on the table. I don't bullshit, and I don't use big words to impress. If I don't agree with you, I'll just tell you. That's my opinion, and I'm entitled to it. Some guys call me the Don Cherry of wagon racing."

He continues, "I don't get along with people who can talk for three hours or three minutes and still do not say anything. I have a problem because I tell people that. I don't care if you own a million-dollar company or sleep under a bridge, I'm no better than you, and you're no better than me. You may have just been a little luckier. I don't think I'm an overly intelligent person or overly educated, I just say it the way it is."

Nevada makes no apologies for himself. "If people don't like me for who I am, then that's just too bad. I try not to swear, which I sometimes have a problem doing, but I do get across how I feel on the subject. I'm not going to kiss anyone's ass. I'll just say it the way it is. I like people who work hard and are straight talkers. If they ever send me to Parliament, holy shit."

Nevada's contributions to wagon racing have included instigating the use of race videotapes, having extra cameras for judging installed, and making countless media appearances. He says, "I worked my ass off, and I wanted the [WPCA Chuckwagon Person of the Year] award. I deserved it — I'm not bragging. I just wanted recognition from my fellow competitors that I did work that hard." Jim also points out, "The award is not voted on by some downtown tie-jockey, it's voted on by people who know the sport and the industry. They picked me, not because I did everything right, but because my heart was there for the sport."

He adds, "I was up against retiring driver Ron David. After I was given the award, his wife, Barb David, came up to me. Barb and I have not always seen eye to eye — in fact, very seldom do we get along — but she gave me a big hug, and her approval was just as good as winning an award."

The off-track awards attest to Nevada's and the cowboys' dedication to and concern for the sport. Wagon racing is highly dependent upon its participants for marketing, growth, and community development. What the cowboys put into the sport, they usually get out of it. Their efforts, silent or noted, are crucial to the sport's vitality.

Brash, outspoken Kelly Sutherland knows the impact and the salvation of quiet victories. Sutherland's most significant conquest occurred noiselessly off the track, alone. On August 24, 1995, in Kennewick, Washington, Sutherland quit drinking alcohol.

His decision ended thirty years of drinking. Sutherland had started "painting his tonsils" when he was fifteen, although he notes, "When I reflect back, I never really had a problem competing with alcohol until 1986, when I was thirty-five." For him, the problem stemmed not just from a love of the taste of beer. "Alcohol is a great depressant and I was always so hyper, sometimes I was way out there in left field. After every wagon race, I slurped down three beers in five minutes. Then I slowed down a little, and each night I drank between twelve and twenty-four beers. In my last year drinking, only three days did I have less than three beers."

"Go hard or go home" aptly describes Sutherland's drinking habits. He says, "I wasn't the guy who could just have one; I was the guy who couldn't leave till the last one was gone. I continually drank till I passed out. Money wasn't a problem. I didn't have a regular job, so I couldn't be fired. If I wanted to get drunk for two or three days, I just jumped in the truck, drove seven hours to Calgary, and did it. No one was there to tell me I couldn't do it. There were no checks and balances. Debbie hated it from day one, but after fifteen years, she quit arguing with me."

Sutherland remains amazed at and grateful for his wife's ability to accommodate him. Sutherland says, "Debbie loves to cook and host people. She would invite people over. Our guests would be waiting while I was out drunk somewhere, then I'd come home half-drunk. That went on continually. If Debbie had been like that, I would have given her a standing taxi pass to the bar. I would have told her, 'Just phone anytime, twenty-four hours a day, but get out of my life.' Why she never ever did that to me is beyond me. I really admire her. It's a miracle I'm still married."

Sutherland was guarded about his drinking, and most people did not realize how much he drank. "I never did it in public, or around corporate people that counted. I got as drunk as anybody can get and act, but I always did it around my family or people I knew." Only once did Sutherland drive his wagon while drunk. He remembers, "Prior to the evening's races, I was in the beer gardens with a couple of old wagon drivers in Wainwright. I already had the show won, but that night I knocked a barrel. I never ever drank before a race again."

The appeal of alcohol nevertheless hobbled Kelly's racing success and transformed the King into a pauper. He humbly recalls, "One time, I bought a bunch of horses in Calgary, and started drinking around noon. That was a bad thing, because everything I did was fast. I drank fast. I'd spent four hundred dollars on the night, which was typical, and I'd left my credit cards and wallet at a nightclub." Fifteen hours later, Sutherland found himself lying half-naked in a convenience store's washroom floor and being awoken by a city cop.

It was 3:30 a.m. The young woman on staff was scared. Sutherland says, "Apparently we asked our taxi to stop so I could use the bathroom. After waiting an hour, the taxi and my buddy left. My friend later said, 'What the hell, we couldn't open the door. I didn't know if you'd gone out the back door and didn't care, it was bedtime.'"

Sutherland got to his feet, sorted his clothes, and the policeman asked him, "What are you doing?" Kelly replied, "I can't tell you, 'cause I can't remember, but I wouldn't be hurting anybody." The officer inquired, "Who are you?" Recognizing Sutherland's name, the policeman asked, "Do you have money? Have you a place to go? You see that cab out there? You get in there or I've got a place for you." Kelly said, "Thank you, pardner," shook his hand, and left.

Looking back at the incident, Sutherland asks himself, "How embarrassed could I be? How would a man ever get himself into that situation? You're not very proud of some of the things that happen when you drink." Sutherland realized alcohol was jeopardizing his businesses and marriage. Booze was also affecting his work ethic around his horses: he was disinterested in wagon racing.

Sutherland's serious soul-searching began after a frightening traffic accident. "I hit another vehicle, but it was empty. I'm not scared to say I was stone drunk and I didn't get charged. I just do not remember hitting that vehicle."

Sutherland remembers the day he quit drinking. "It was just as if a light switch came on. I woke up that morning and said, 'I'll never drink another drop as long as I will live.' I just became full. A lot of other people still drinking have not had enough, and when they have had enough they'll quit, the only thing is they might be in a box when it happens. I like it on this side of the dirt."

When Kelly no longer drank four to five hours a day, Debbie was astounded. And his horses began to see more of him. Sutherland now had the time to focus on training and driving, which led him to his Calgary Stampede trophies in 1997, 1998, and 1999, and his World championship wins in 1996, 1998, and 1999. He says, "I know if I hadn't quit drinking, I couldn't have achieved what I did."

Winning the WPCA and CPCA tour championships are the cowboys' season-long goals. Those cowboys belonging to the WPCA compete for the World championship, and the cowboys who are members of the CPCA compete for that association's championship. These championships are awarded to the drivers only, with separate end-of-season awards given to the outriders. Sutherland says of the circuit titles, "Compared to the Stampede, the World champion is actually judged highest by our peers. It is awarded to the most consistent outfit over the year." By 1999, Sutherland had won a record eight World championships. Bensmiller, who switched to the WPCA circuit in 1996, won the title in 1997; prior to the move, he won the CPCA title eight times.

Nevada's, Bensmiller's, and Sutherland's title victories are cinched to their belts. Wagon cowboys do not need to crow — the polished saucer-sized silver and gold trophy buckles speak for themselves. The buckles' glimmer details the cowboys' pluck, their expertise, and their horsemanship. Amongst the cowboy society, and especially to the boyfriend-chasing "buckle bunnies," the silver speaks volumes.

Yet Jim Nevada feels the buckles really matter only to the cowboys who get to take them home. To most of the world, a chuckwagon championship is meaningless. He says, "Chuckwagon drivers are a hero for ten days in Calgary, but the rest of the time we're just some Joe Shmuck cowboy. You see some guys walking around like a peacock, but no one notices you. Some wagon drivers don't realize [they're] not a household name."

Despite the lack of fame and having already won Calgary six times as an outrider, Jim Nevada still wants, for his own satisfaction, to win the Rangeland Derby as a driver. Nevada feels he has been luckier than most cowboys, but he wants to be even luckier. He notes, "I don't sit and fantasize about holding the fifty-thousand-dollar cheque. I suppose my fantasies might be different, if I hadn't been on the stage so much as an outrider."

As Nevada has stated, the buckles just hold up the cowboys' faded Wrangler jeans. A cowboy can only wear one belt, and most of the trophy buckles end up on a dusty shelf or at the back of the sock drawer. The real proof of the cowboys' accomplishments shines in their eyes and their poise. The criteria for success can vary, and only the cowboys know if they have attained a true victory. The verdicts passed by the racetrack judges are not nearly as conclusive as the verdicts the cowboys pass on themselves. The cowboys know themselves what they deserve, and what they have won.

CHAPTER 7

The Spokes of Fate

I was fifteen years old, it was my second show outriding, and I was nervous. Veteran driver Orville Strandquist said to me, "Jim, when your card's laid, it's played. It could be on the racetrack or in a car on your way to Calgary, but as long as you're doing something you like, that's what you do. You don't know when you're going to die, and don't push it, but when your card's played, you're dead."

After that I was never nervous.

JIM NEVADA

Accidents and injury ride shotgun with every chuckwagon. In the careening squall of horses and men, the potential for physical and emotional pain is ever-present. Pain can come in many forms: the sharp pangs of breaking a rib, the despair of hearing a horse's leg break, the grief of seeing a cowboy die on the track. But the cowboys do not allow themselves to be crippled by the threat of pain. They respect and accept the dangers inherent in chuckwagon racing, whether those dangers lurk in the barns, behind the barrels, or down the backstretch. They understand that the sport they love may someday break their heart.

The tragedies usually occur when wagons, horses, and cowboys collide on the track. Wrecks may result from faulty equipment, cowboy error, injured horses, unfavourable weather or track conditions, or simple misfortune. They can be unpredictable, and at times unavoidable.

Over the years, many wrecks have been attributed to the type of equipment used. Like many human endeavours, wagon racing has been reactive rather than proactive. Wagon racing was founded on western heritage, and the spirit of rugged and wily teamsters racing on the plains lingers. Unfortunately, the devotion to heritage and tradition — in preference to ensuring that equipment is changed for safety — has led to injured cowboys and horses.

An example is the fifty-pound wooden stove. Kelly Sutherland explains, "The whole sport hinged around tradition, rough and tumble. That stove was the stupidest goddam thing in the world. When your outrider failed to load that stove, it was left lying in the dirt. The wagon turned the top barrel, and what was sitting in its path by the bottom barrel? It's a square box, as big as a footstool weighing fifty pounds. You went right over top of it. It upset wagons and horses fell." Jim Nevada agrees, "That stove was just asking for some pain."

The racing committees did not want to change the stove's design, rationalizing it would alter the fundamentals of wagon racing. Sutherland argues, "When they designed the stove in the 1930s, they didn't have no goddam thoroughbreds that started. With thoroughbreds, if you had a fast-starting outfit, the stove man couldn't get the stove in, so you were penalized for being too fast."

After numerous horses and wagons crashed into the impenetrable stove, the crushable ten-pound rubber stoves were eventually developed. For the cowboys, it was a welcome safety improvement. Loading the new stove has been retained as a task for the outriders, but the task is no longer insurmountable.

For safety reasons, many outriders and some drivers are also now wearing protective vests, similar to ones worn by roughstock rodeo riders. Bensmiller says, "I would never wear a flak jacket, but my son Kurt is going to wear one. He can't drive without one, training or anything — I won't let him. I know that's not the right way to look at it — I won't wear it and he has to — but I'm the boss." Bensmiller adds, "I'm from the old school. I still don't do up my seat belt. I don't need it."

Mastering wagon racing, and particularly outriding, is a college of hard knocks. Jim Nevada recounts one mishap he had as an outrider. "One year Randy Robinson and I piled up in Grande Prairie. Tyler Helmig was a new driver, and he dropped his lines into the wheels. The lines became caught and Helmig's horses were pulled to the right. Tyler and the other two wagons were pushed to the outside, and they ran through the anchor link fence.

"Randy and I were on the outside and we couldn't get out of the wreck. Randy's horse hit the fence, fell, and landed on top of Randy's legs. When I hit, I went flying overtop the fence. They paced it off later — and I flew forty feet through the air, fifteen feet high. I remember looking down at Randy in slow motion. I hit the ground and was knocked out."

Nevada adds as an aside, "Apparently, as I laid on the ground, my helmet had come off. A lady came out of the grandstand, grabbed my helmet and outriding bat, and turned to walk away. Tara Cosgrave stopped her and asked, 'Excuse me, what are you doing with that?' The woman replied, 'Well, he won't need it any more.'"

Nevada was rushed to the hospital. "I didn't recall anything until I woke up in the ambulance. I had a neck brace on, and tape all over me. I thought, 'Shit, I'm paralyzed.' Things started to clear up for me when I was in the hospital. I laid there and I wiggled my fingers, 'Alright, I'm okay,' then I wiggled my toes, 'Shit, great!' So I snapped the tape off my arms and legs and got up."

It had been raining that evening during the races, and Nevada was covered in mud. He took off his neck brace and wet clothes, and started washing the blood and dirt off his face. He recalls, "Nobody was coming around. So I sat down and lit a smoke. A nurse came in and snaps, 'Put the smoke out!' She then asked, 'Where's the patient?' I told her I was the patient. She said, 'Get the hell back in that bed right now.' I told her, 'Clean [the bed] up first.' She retorted, 'Get the hell back in there.'"

Nevada resumes, "So I put the brace back on, and I laid down in the sand and mud. The doctor who showed up might as well have been a veterinarian — he was terrible. They sent me for x-rays, and I was okay. That was the only time they got me into an ambulance."

Buddy Bensmiller was also forced into an ambulance during his years as an outrider. As Bensmiller was charging down the homestretch, his horse broke its neck just before the finish line. "She fell on top of me and I couldn't get out," he describes.

"Another wagon was coming around the turn and he ran over the mare, ripping up muscles in my leg. If the mare hadn't been lying on me, the wagon would have run over me. I didn't even want to get in the ambulance, but it was the last race and I felt I could get out of doing chores."

Outriders are not the only cowboys to get tossed around the track. Kelly Sutherland watched Rupert Fisher, a wagon driver from Duck Lake, Saskatchewan, take an uncontrolled ride. Sutherland says, "We were racing in Bonnyville, Alberta. Ray Croteau came out wide around the bottom barrel, and his lead team knocked the back end of Fisher's box off of the wheel frame. The front end was still pinned through by a hinge pin. Every time Fisher pulled his lines, the box swung around on top of the horses, and every time he let go, the box fell down between the wheels. He didn't know what to do."

Sutherland and George Normand were sitting in their wagons behind the track, waiting to race. Sutherland says, "Fisher decides to tie the lines around the seat. He gets out and walks down the reach. He was walking a skinny plank at forty miles an hour. I said to George, 'Watch this. You want to see a guy trying to die?' Fisher made two steps, and off he went. The wagon wheel hit him hard, and he tumbled for about a hundred metres down the track. Fisher got up. There was nothing wrong with that son of a bitch. I've never seen anything like that in my life."

Sooner or later, all drivers discover firsthand what it feels like to fly out of a wagon. At Calgary, Bensmiller's line got hung up. As his outfit was going around the top barrel, the line to the right-hand leader got caught in the right-hand wheel horse's bridle. The line could not slip, and after Bensmiller turned the barrel, rather than turning left on the bottom barrel, his horses kept turning to the right.

Bensmiller recounts what happened next, "I crashed and was thrown out. I tore my shoulder out, and my outfit ran away. As I stood there, one of my outriders came by, so I told him to get off his horse. I jumped on, and that put my shoulder back in, but I just about fell off." He continues, "When I caught up to my outfit, the horses were stopped. They took me to the hospital and told me I was facing two months of recovery. In three days I was back driving. The last night, I outrode for Bruce Craige, and we won the Stampede, but I had to jump on the opposite side of the horse."

The drivers need to keep calm, regardless of the confusion surrounding them. Their horses rely upon their directions. If the horses sense that their driver is panicking, or that their driver lacks control, then runaways and accidents are prone to happen. Sutherland describes, "If you have emotional peaks and valleys when you're driving, you lose your strength. I've seen cowboys big enough to lift a pickup truck, but when they had the lines, they couldn't pull a piece of straw across a bale. Mostly, it is because they're scared."

Yet no matter how confident the drivers are, wrecks can happen anywhere and at any time — even during practice. "At Wainwright, Alberta," remembers Sutherland, "Joe King took the worst ride I've ever seen a man take. He was practising in the morning, and his wagon pole's draw pin fell out. Only the stay chains still held the pole.

"Somebody screamed, guys were saddling horses, and we knew there was going to be a wreck like no tomorrow. The wagon started to go sideways till it was almost backwards, and then the chain broke. The wagon came around the far turn, dug right into the dirt, pitching Joe out fifty feet. He landed on his head in the dirt."

Joe King lived to talk about the crash, but Sutherland considers, "That was the scariest wagon wreck I've ever seen. I'll tell you, after that I checked my pole before every trip."

Track maintenance errors can pose another hazard for the cowboys. In his second year of driving, Bensmiller was thrown into a nasty pileup owing to such an error. He was racing at Battleford, Saskatchewan. The track had been watered, but the watering truck had not been shut off and a dangerous slick spot had resulted. "I was out in front by four lengths," says Bensmiller. "My leader slipped on the water, broke her shoulder, and as my wagon slid sideways, Stu Napper and Maynard Metchewais piled into me." He continues, "Stu went at least fourteen feet into the air, right over the plywood fence. Maynard was at the back and he saw the wreck coming, so he dropped to his knees in the bottom of his wagon box. He flew straight out, taking the dashboard right off.

"There were only two horses left standing, yet I only lost one horse, and all the rest were all right. Stu was shaken up, but unhurt. Both of Maynard's legs were broken, he tore a kneecap off, and had nightmares for months. It was a year and a half before Maynard could walk, and three years before he drove again."

The threat of accidents can be nightmare fodder for the cowboys' families. The people who love the cowboys are often more apprehensive than the cowboys themselves. Jim Nevada says, "The danger don't bug me, but half the time, my wife is a nervous wreck. The night before a race in Ponoka, Kim dreamt I made the finals, but in the race I rolled my wagon, was hit, and impaled on a post. At the time, she didn't tell me her dream."

Coincidentally, Nevada made the finals at Ponoka. He recalls the race, "I was out of shape on the barrels, and I rolled [the wagon] on the first turn. Kim saw me having problems, but at the first turn there is a concession stand blocking the view, and she didn't see me roll. She ran to the first turn and here comes my wagon upside down. She thinks, 'Holy shit, my dream came true.' She was stunned."

At the time, Nevada's first thought was for the wagon, which had been loaned to him. He explains, "I had borrowed Richard Cosgrave's wagon, and he told me, 'Don't roll it.' Well, I went out there and rolled it. Busted the seat off of it, busted it all up."

Nevada pulled himself up and went over to Cosgrave to give him part of the broken seat. Nevada was scheduled to outride in the next race, so he then walked over to Kim, who was holding his outriding helmet. She handed him his helmet, and he jumped on his outriding horse. Nevada remembers, "I looked at her, and she was glassy-eyed. She wasn't there. She still had not told me her dream. She thought when that wagon came around, she would go back and find me imbedded on a post."

Jim was worried. Kim was driving home alone that night, so he phoned Kim's parents that evening and told them, "You better take care of your daughter. I had a little wreck up here." Kim returned home in tears. Jim says, "Her parents finally settled her down, but the Ponoka Stampede highlights were on TV, and the first thing they showed was me flipping out. Well, she broke down again."

In the chuckwagon community, there is no greater sadness than when a competitor is killed. The 1990s were a solemn decade, as three drivers and one outrider died in wagon accidents. In the small wagon community, no one was untouched by grief.

In 1993, thirty-six-year-old driver Richard Cosgrave was killed at a race in Kamloops, British Columbia. Richard was the son of two-time Stampede champion Bob Cosgrave and grandson of ten-time Stampede champion Dick Cosgrave. He was also a husband and father. One of the most personable wagon drivers of his generation, Richard simply loved wagon racing.

Kelly Sutherland was in the same heat as Cosgrave when the accident occurred. "It was a freak thing," says Sutherland, describing the events. "He was on Barrel 1, I was on 2, and Norm Cuthbertson was on 3. We turned together, side by side, and just as I turned the bottom barrel, his right front wheel broke off. It looked like his wagon was going to upset. I had out-turned him, so I drifted fifteen to twenty feet away. His wagon lifted, lifted, and then came back down. He kind of froze, looking at me. Meanwhile, his runaway wheel rolled right down the centre of Norm's lead team. How it missed knocking down the horses, I don't know."

Sutherland continues, "Richard moved to get up on the seat. A hundred yards from the infield, the wagon jumped over a mound of dirt, flipping him out of the box. Richard landed hanging outside of the box. His feet were hooked up underneath the seat, and he hung with his nose right on the ground. His face was going to hit the ground, so he put his hands down into the dirt and he was sucked out of the wagon. Lying on the ground, he was turned around, and the back wheel ran over his chest, cutting the aorta off to his heart."

Sutherland speculates that had Cosgrave been thrown away from his own wagon, he likely would not have been injured. Cosgrave's wagon had sturdy steel axles, but the accident was attributed to a fault in the steel's fabrication. Following the accident, the drivers insisted that all wagons be constructed by an approved builder, and wagon inspections are now mandatory.

A race from the first evening of the 1999 Calgary Stampede is perhaps the most televised chuckwagon race in history. Unfortunately, chuckwagons are considered worthy of international news coverage only when a spectacular mishap occurs at the Stampede. That evening's tragic events led to a black mark being unjustly placed on the sport. News footage and editorials on the accident merely reinforced the stereotype of wagon racing as an excessively dangerous novelty sport, and the cowboys as thrill-seekers.

The race video shows Larry McEwan's outfit on the rail position, leading down the backstretch. Behind him raced Ron David, followed by Bill McEwan, Larry's father. Larry McEwan's wagon shifted away from the rail to the right. As it did, Ron David's left-wheel horse fell, causing his wagon to go sideways. Bill McEwan's wagon collided with David's wagon, and both Ron David and Bill McEwan were thrown out of their wagons. Two trailing outriders were hurt when their horses collided with the back of Ron David's flipping wagon.

Reviewing the accident, Kelly Sutherland says, "Usually when a horse is hit by a wagon, its running stride is interrupted, and its head goes up, and then down. That didn't happen. To me it looks like Ronnie's horse broke its leg. Ronnie's was horse running, and then — slam — he broke a leg or dropped dead from a heart attack." He continues, "If his horse did have a heart attack, usually they don't drop right away. Instead the horse will stagger awhile — the horse's momentum keeps it going maybe one hundred yards. I've had that happen, where a horse is actually dead but still running and then they stop, crater, and don't kick once. But Ronnie's horse just dropped."

Sutherland continues, "Either way, when the horse falls and stops Ronnie's wagon, Bill McEwan tries to duck around at forty miles per hour. He goes round to the outside, but just hooks his back axle with the back end of Ronnie's wagon, throwing Ronnie out. Everything stops dead for a second, and Bill is shot out of the wagon like a cannon, driving his head down into the dirt and crushing his skull."

Eventually, the judges faulted Larry McEwan for pulling his horses out from the rail as he looked over his shoulder. Examining the chain of events, Bensmiller says, "They say Larry's wagon jumped out six inches, clipping Ron's horse. And there's no doubt it did." But Bensmiller believes Larry McEwan was unfairly blamed. "A horse changes strides as they come out of a turn and go down the stretch. Some of them take a while to change, and when they do, the wagon shifts whichever way that horse changes."

Buddy emphasizes, "There ain't one wagon that will go straight down the backstretch. They catch a rut or the horse changes stride, and the wagons move. Just because it happened at that instant, they blamed the accident on Larry. It wasn't his fault. We all run tight, so it ain't Ronnie's fault either. Some point in a race you end up too close, it just happens. It was just one of them things you couldn't do anything about — an act of God. There's definitely no changing it now, and I don't know what you could've done to change it then."

Ron David was seriously hurt, and his left-wheel horse was euthanized. Bill McEwan clung to life-support systems for two days before dying. Three days after the accident, the Calgary Stampede and the chuckwagon community held a ceremony prior to the evening's wagon races to celebrate Bill's life. With drivers, outriders, and families lining the track, Larry McEwan drove his father's wagon into the infield. Cowboys held their hats to their hearts and bowed their heads. That evening, Larry McEwan stoically returned to wagon racing.

In the Stampede barns, a simple memorial for Bill sprung up on hay bales placed in front of his tack room. Photographs, flowers, cards, his belt, and his helmet and goggles were placed on the hay. For the rest of the Stampede, Larry drove his father's wagon as well as his own, flags were hung at half-mast, and drivers wore purple armbands — the colours of Bill's rig.

Kelly Sutherland notes, "You couldn't stage an accident like that, especially halfway down the backstretch. Sometimes you've got to be a little fatalistic. It must have been meant to be; otherwise how the hell would it have happened?" He adds, "The wagons are goddam safe now, but nothing gives. We changed to steel construction because the wagons and axles were breaking when turning. But when the wooden wagons were in a wreck, and you hit a wheel or an axle, the axle could break or tear off." The wagons disintegrated spectacularly, and bones were broken, but rarely were lives lost.

The McEwan wreck also highlighted the outriders' vulnerability. In any wagon race, outriders run the greater risk of breaking legs and arms. Kelly Sutherland explains, "In that wreck, you can see two outriders going for a terrible ride. They're going through the air, and their horses are going overtop. They couldn't see the wreck coming. They were going hell-bent for leather, and when they could see it, it was too late."

For many outriders, such hazards motivate them to retire from outriding. The sagacity of age replaces the indestructibility of youth. Sutherland acknowledges, "That's the reason I quit outriding: I got scared. I no longer felt a hundred percent secure on a horse. I started thinking, 'If the horse goes down, I'm going to get hurt,' and as soon as you start that, you ain't going to make it. However, I always feel really secure in a wagon, like I'm in a protective cage there. The only time I don't is when you tip over, and it's always the guys behind that end up getting you."

Immediately following the McEwan accident, wagon racing was attacked for its dangers and its cruelty to horses. The accusations were an affront to the grieving cowboys.

The media approached Jim Nevada, Ron David's friend, to report his and the cowboys' perspective. Nevada comments, "I'd done an interview a couple of days before, and I had really [gone] to work trying to defend the horses and drivers, explaining to people that the horses don't have a choice, but what animal does? They did not use any of my quotes. They used one sentence of mine, and gave an animal-rights guy thirty seconds of air time. The piece was fricken one-sided. That's when I lost it with the media."

With Ron David hurt, a replacement driver was needed to drive his wagon for the rest of the Stampede. Nevada agreed to do so, and each evening he drove both his own wagon and David's. It was stressful and exhausting for Jim, especially since his outfit was among the leaders. One evening was especially trying. "My arms were so tired, they felt about thirty inches longer than normal," he relates. "Plus on the racetrack, Kelly was playing some mind games on me. Afterwards, coming off the track, he and I had a four-letter conversation."

Arriving back in the barns, Nevada encountered a television interviewer with a camera crew. Jim says, "I was sick of this interviewer from Toronto telling me all he knew about wagon racing, when he wasn't smart enough to cut the goddam whistle off his cowboy hat."

Nevada was put on live, and without the broadcasters being able to edit his comments, he said point-blank, "People out East don't know shit about wagon racing. They don't know a chuckwagon from the little red wagon they pulled as a kid. They don't know a pinto from a thoroughbred." He added, "They haven't been back to the barns to see how hard we work. We take care of these horses; we cry when they get hurt. The only time the media rushes out is when there is a wreck and they have no clue about the sport."

A friend in Toronto telephoned Jim the next week and agreed, "You're right, we don't know shit about wagons." Nevada said to him, "It drives me nuts. People tell me all about my sport, who don't know a goddam thing."

Looking back on the statements he made, Nevada says, "I was still rattled from arguing with Kelly. I knew what I wanted to say, but it didn't come out the right way. I had an all-round bad day."

In light of his remarks before the media, Jim recalls how stunned he was when his name was announced for the Guy Weadick Memorial Award. "I thought I had a snowball's chance in hell to win the Guy Weadick. Maybe fighting for the cowboys was a turning point." Nevada's no-nonsense comments and frank cowboy pride were needed to defend the sport against misinformed and prejudiced judgements.

Despite the dangers in wagon racing, there have actually been relatively few fatalities during the races. In total, only ten cowboys have died during professional chuckwagon races throughout the history of the sport.

The Calgary Stampede has witnessed five deaths in its seventy-seven years of running wagon races. In 1948, spectator Eddy Swain died while running out onto the track to meet his brother John, who had just won the Stampede; Eddy was hit by a late outriding horse. In 1960, driver Don Chapin was killed when his wagon overturned. In 1971, outrider Rod Glass was tossed to his death. Then for twenty-five years Calgary saw no more fatalities, until outrider Eugene Jackson died from head injuries suffered during the 1996 Calgary Stampede. And in 1999, Bill McEwan died.

Chuckwagon fatalities that have occurred at Cheyenne, Wyoming, include Rod Bullock in 1960, driver Gordie Bridge in 1971, and outrider Randy Evans (Buddy Bensmiller's friend) in 1986.

And in addition to Richard Cosgrave's death in 1993, there was the one other fatality in the 1990s: George Normand, who was killed in 1994. Buddy Bensmiller again learned how much chuckwagon racing gives and takes. To Bensmiller and the other cowboys' credit, they make the most of the life they are given, and there are no regrets if it suddenly ends. Even when it is the life of their best friend.

George Normand and Buddy Bensmiller shared their infatuation for horses with each other, from pony chariot racing to professional wagon racing. Bensmiller says, "George loved wagon horses, just like me. In the spring, he usually built a racetrack at his place, so I'd take my horses up there and train. We raced together, giving new horses the experience of competition, finding out together [which] horses blew up or lost their mind."

Their friendship endured, even though they raced in rival associations: Normand in the WPCA and Bensmiller in the CPCA. Their circuits took them to different towns and cities, which meant they saw each other infrequently during the summer. But they did meet to race at the Calgary Stampede. Although they followed different paths, their mutual allegiance was to the sport.

"George was pretty good with horses," Bensmiller reflects. "He wasn't what you'd call a teamster, but he could sure drive a wagon. He had a good feel for horses, and was a caretaker. George definitely looked after his horses, and the last few years all he did was horses."

On July 2, 1994, at the Ponoka Stampede, George Normand had drawn the tight-turning Barrel 1. Bensmiller recalls the race. "He had a bad horse, one I told him he should have canned a long time ago, but he liked him too well. That was his biggest fault: if he liked a horse too much, it could do nothing wrong. From the start of the race, the horse was fighting him; it was raining, and he just couldn't get hold of his lines. He made a bad turn at the top barrel, got out of shape, and by the bottom barrel he was really out of shape."

Kelly Sutherland also remembers the race. "We were using those old stiff barrels," he notes. "The barrel bucked the front end of Normand's wagon, pitching George on the seat, and as he turned onto the track, the barrel hit his back axle. George was thrown out and under the wheels of another wagon."

Buddy watched the accident unfold from only yards away. "I don't know why, but that night I stood in the infield. Usually I stand up on the fence and watch, but for some reason that night I walked in. He says, "I was the first one to George when he was dying. He was trying to get up, but he was badly hurt. He looked around but couldn't say much. They say he was alive when they loaded him into the ambulance, but I don't think he was."

Bensmiller reflects, "It always takes a tragedy to make changes. It's the same thing with those goddam barrels. I told George for years, 'Those rubber barrels are too hard. You hit them wrong, they'll upset you, and they'll kill somebody.' George was the one who ran over one. If it wasn't for them barrels, George would still be alive." Collapsible barrels are now compulsory.

Looking back, Bensmiller believes Normand seemed to act differently from normal prior to the fateful race. Buddy says, "I had my horses in Hobbema. The morning before the race, George phoned to check to see if I was coming to the races that night. I said, 'Why, what do you need?' George asked, 'What time are you coming?' 'About 6 p.m.,' I replied. George said, 'I just wanted to make sure you're coming.' I asked, 'Do you need something?' He said, 'Nope, I just wanted to make sure you were there.'"

Bensmiller adds, "Similarly, when Randy Evans was killed in Cheyenne, he came to visit while we were having supper before the race. I asked Randy if he wanted a bite to eat, and usually he'd grab something. But Randy said, 'I had a half a cantaloupe — that's all I've eaten today. I don't feel right. I feel empty inside.' We never thought anything of it.

"It just seems like those guys know something is going to happen. They change. I don't believe in superstition or that kind of shit, but with both of them guys, they just weren't right the day that it happened."

A week after Normand's accident, Bensmiller drove his and George's wagons all ten days at the Calgary Stampede. After the Stampede, Normand's wagons and horses were auctioned off, but before they were sold, Buddy attached George's lucky chrome steer heads to his wagon.

As devastating as this tragedy was, Bensmiller did not second-guess wagon racing. He states, "George was definitely doing something that he loved. I'd say he loved wagon racing more than anybody. He loved it all. There ain't too many things you can do in this world and make a living at it, that you really love to do. Not too many of us get lucky enough to be able to do that.

"A flak jacket may have saved George, or maybe he would be in a wheelchair — so as far as I'm concerned he's better off where he's at."

Bensmiller and Normand recognized the sport's perils. They accepted their chosen risks. Buddy adds, "Especially after Richard Cosgrave died, we always talked about getting killed. We figured we'd go in a car wreck in the middle of the night somewhere — I guess I probably still will. He ain't going to."

Luck and destiny: they guide a wagon driver. And the cowboys chart their course with bravado. To grab the reins minutes after watching a friend be loaded into an ambulance takes devotion, concentration, and foolhardiness. Jim Nevada suggests, "Anybody who wants to hook up four thoroughbreds to a thirteen-hundred-pound buggy has got to have a few marbles loose."

When Kelly Sutherland travels into the United States, even people who know little about chuckwagons are aware of the fatalities. Kelly says, "The first questions posed are 'Aren't you scared?' 'Is it dangerous?' 'What happens when you have a wreck?'"

Sutherland responds, "To anyone who is competing, those questions are a non-issue. The wrecks certainly happen, there's no denying it. It's like driving a race car — it goes with the territory."

He adds, "The fatalities are unsettling to people away from the sport and within it. I don't spend a lot of time dwelling on that, because if you did, you wouldn't drive a wagon. For me, I'm in a sport that comes very easy for me, very naturally. I'm driven to do it, and whatever happens, happens. It's quite unique I could make a living out of something so easy, so natural. I feel blessed or very fortunate with that."

Sutherland believes wagon drivers are makers of their own fate and he does not feel he is jumping onto a widow-maker each race. "At least you're the guy who can control the chain of events," he points out. "Every fatality I have witnessed, or understood the circumstances, has been avoidable. However, all the drivers made choices I would've made. If you are a very, very avid competitor, you are going to make borderline choices all the time, trying to win. If you don't take a gamble, you won't ever have a sniff of winning, and even if you do gamble, lots of times you don't win.

"It's quite ironic the sport now has more safety features than we thought possible, and it is when we're having the fatalities. That troubles me. I think it has to do with guys buying better livestock and going faster. I don't know if the skill level is keeping up — I know it isn't."

Jim Nevada agrees, "The sport is safer, but it is getting faster." He adds, "The deaths the last few years are kind of a fluke thing, 'cause for fifteen years when I was a kid no one died. We had some wrecks that looked a hundred times worse, when no one was killed." In the history of wagon racing, the frequency of fatalities in the 1990s was abnormal.

Buddy Bensmiller believes there are no simple reasons behind the accidents. "Some people say the speed is causing the accidents. Maybe speed affects the seriousness of the accident, but I don't think that's what's causing it. How many times do we go around the racetrack when things should happen, but they don't?"

When people challenge Jim Nevada's chosen lifestyle, he asks, "What ain't dangerous in a sport now? Look at how many football and hockey players have concussions." Both Nevada and Bensmiller also agree that they would rather drive a wagon than drive their pickups down Calgary's Deerfoot Trail. Buddy says, "It's scarier out in the traffic as far as I'm concerned."

Nevada adds, "I look at other sports like auto racing, and I think they are as crazy as us. You see some people in car accidents: the cars are demolished, and they walk away. They should've been in a body bag. Sometimes, though, you see cars hardly banged up and there is a person dead. Wagon racing is a dangerous sport, but we've had people die who shouldn't have died — it was just a fluke." He continues, "You're always going to have wrecks in horse sports, whether it's horse racing or jiggy-joggers [harness racing]. You never hear about a pacer race until there's a pileup. We're only newsworthy when there are horses, drivers, and outriders flying everywhere. People who watch the national news think this is a common occurrence, but from 1999, the last time there was a big wreck was in 1986."

Bensmiller typifies the cowboys' approach to chuckwagon racing's threats. "I've never been scared," he says. "I always figured if a guy was scared, he shouldn't be there. If you're scared, then things are going to happen. I know a lot of people think I'm full of shit when I say it, but I've never really found anything to be scared of."

Buddy's wife, Darlene, also has faith in her husband. Buddy remarks, "I asked my wife one time if she ever worries about me, and she said she worries about the other guys more than me. She has confidence in my abilities — just not confidence in the other guys' abilities."

Bensmiller concludes, "I'm a firm believer that when it's your day to go, you're going to go. I don't care whether you're driving a truck or driving a wagon. Your days are numbered, and that's when it's going to happen."

It takes special individuals — the men, their wives and girlfriends, their families — to continue to love a sport that can offer so much sorrow. To cope with the tragedies, Bensmiller, Nevada, and Sutherland do not profess any strong religious beliefs; instead they take comfort in knowing that the cowboys died doing what they dreamed of doing. If these men had their choice, they would not want it any other way.

By continuing to compete, they are not disregarding the wrecks, and especially not devaluing their friends who were killed. Rather, their efforts are their eulogy; they race to celebrate and remember those cowboys. Out of respect, the races must go on.

This "cowboy philosophy" is realistic and pragmatic. For spectators, it may be difficult to comprehend how the cowboys can reconcile the hazards. However, the cowboys appreciate there are risks in life, no matter what trail any cowboy or cowgirl rides. These men simply have the remarkable character, and the privilege, to live their lives to the full while they can. Far from being questionable, their resolute character is admirable.

RON DAVID'S CHUCKWAGON PRAYER

Here we are again today
Risking our lives for very little pay -
But it's the life we choose
And the life we shall live,
And Lord we don't ask anyone to give.
But we just want to Thank You
For the many trouble free miles we travel each year;
Up and down the highways and dusty old roads
Knowing that you're near.
Now, we ain't always been straight,
Or taken a religious stand,
But when we crawl upon the seat of that wagon
And look back at the family,
There's someone we truly believe in
And you're the Man.
And when we turn them barrels
And she lifts up on two,
I sometimes hear a little voice saying,
"Don't worry son, 'cause I'm in here too."
In the past you have taken a few drivers
And a few outriders, even the odd child or two;
But really, Lord, no one has really ever blamed you.
So we don't ask that you take us to Heaven,
Or never run in stormy weather,
But when it's all over
And you gather us into your mighty Kingdom Come
Would you please keep us
All together.

AMEN

Driver Ron David wrote this poem around 1980, when he was goin' down the road in an old truck. David says, "We had lots of time travelling in that truck." He has recited the poem wherever wagon people gather, but laughs, "Let's just say it's used more at funerals than weddings." David adds, "I knew it off by heart before I even put it on paper."

CHAPTER 8

Following Heroes

I've always said, the best part of wagon racing is you get to race against your heroes, but the worst part is the same thing. To be a champion, you've got to beat your heroes.

MARK SUTHERLAND

Around the globe, boys and girls admire and emulate professional sports stars. They are the children's role models. In pro chuckwagon racing, young men also strive to be and compete like their heroes, only often their hero is their uncle or father. Aside from exceptional cowboys like Jim Nevada, most wagon drivers are raised within chuckwagon or horse-minded families. The wagon ruts that the new generations chase were left by the men who love them and raised them.

Chuckwagon racing operates on a generational cycle. Every twenty to twenty-five years, another core group of men enters the circuit. Throughout the sport's history, this pattern has been followed. Wagon cowboys, unlike some athletes, can compete essentially their entire adult lives (they are forced to retire from competition only at age sixty-five). As these cowboys keep racing, they are training and competing against their protégés.

At the beginning of the twenty-first century, wagon racing experienced a rebirth with the arrival of the fourth generation. A group of competitive and assertive young men has recently entered the wagon infields. These men are poised to challenge the seemingly indomitable veterans like Buddy Bensmiller and Kelly Sutherland. They are the young guns.

Yet before the eager cowboys are rewarded the lines and accepted as worthy successors, they must prove themselves. Ever since cowboys have saddled up to ride, greenhorns have had to face hurdles and tests. Today's young, passionate chuckwagon drivers must demonstrate that they possess the required horsemanship, canny driving skills, and confidence — attributes that are still respected and revered on the western plains.

The name Dorchester resonates with the rumbling of chuckwagons. Amiable Troy Dorchester is well aware of the obstacles to becoming a chuckwagon champion, as well as the family responsibility. His father — Garry Dorchester — and his uncle Dallas Dorchester, both won Calgary Stampede titles; and Troy's grandfather, Tom Dorchester, also won two Stampede Rangeland Derbies and was one of the pillars of the sport.

Born in 1972, Troy is robust and built like a solid hay bale. His kindness and fondness for horses found a kindred spirit in his new bride, Jennifer Kachor. Troy Dorchester is renowned for his good nature and his hearty chuckle — a laugh that rings right through the barns day and night.

Mark Sutherland, Kelly Sutherland's only son, is the heir to the title "King." Mark has large cowboy boots to fill, as he faces the public expectation that he will win like his father. Born in 1971, Mark is one of the few drivers who is a university graduate, holding an undergraduate degree in education. Mark is well spoken, and his teaching degree reflects his concern for the broad community. He is dedicated to his wife, Dina, and their two young children. Mark considers himself to be a late-blooming driver, despite having savoured some success early in his career.

These two men are examples of the new wave of drivers. They represent the cowboys who will carry the sport into the first quarter of the twenty-first century. Troy and Mark were born into the sport. Surrounded by the chuckwagons, the horses, and the wagon community as they grew up, wagon racing became a passion they were destined to follow.

One of Troy Dorchester's earliest memories is driving his dad's chuckwagon in the Calgary Stampede parade. He was only five or six years old, but he was already standing between his father's legs, driving the team.

Unlike for most children, "playing chuckwagon" was a natural part of Dorchester's western childhood. He reminisces, "When we were young, my cousin Quinn and I tied binder twine to our belt loops, ran around pop cans for barrels, and made a straight run to a finish line. One guy was the horse, and one was the driver. We played hours doing that.

"When we were older," he adds, "most kids played football or ball hockey, but we'd get on our pedal bikes and go wagon race. Quinn usually outrode and I was the driver. He had to jump on his bike and be within a certain length of mine, so he wasn't 'late.'" The games paid off, as Quinn has evolved into an exceptional outrider. In '91, '93, and '95, Quinn was a Calgary Stampede champion outrider, and in '99, he was the WPCA champion outrider.

Troy's grandfather, Tom — the family's patriarch — inspired him to follow the wagons. Troy says, "Pretty much my grandpa is my idol. He made our family name to what it is in wagon racing. As a kid I did a lot with him almost every day. I galloped his horses, and he got me seriously hooked on thoroughbreds." Troy watched his grandfather and his uncles Dallas Dorchester and Dave Lewis race and win the Calgary Stampede; and he grew up hoping to imitate their success.

Similarly, Mark Sutherland was initiated into the sport when he was a child. His father played an influential role. "For me," states Mark, "when you grow up around the intensity of my dad and learn how important the sport is to him, it's inevitable that it's going to become a major part of your life."

All year round, Sutherland's childhood revolved around wagons and horses, but the exceptional memories were formed at the Calgary Stampede. He recalls, "One time, I was pretty young, but old enough to hold dad's lead team in the chute [the lineup area where the four wagons sit before being called onto the racetrack]. At that time, the barns were over across the river, different than where they are now.

"I went over with Dad — and he was, as usual, sitting in the standings high enough to make the finals. We were crossing the bridge when an older horse, who knew better, decided to throw a wreck. Basically the horse was just feeling fresh, and was jumpin', buckin', and kickin'. The horse kicked over his tugs. He got caught up, laid down, and started squealin'. It was just Dad and I, and about two hundred spectators."

Mark and Kelly were in a pickle. The Calgary Stampede's rules state that if a chuckwagon outfit is not ready to compete when the race is scheduled to start, the race starts without the outfit. "They don't stop for anybody," says Mark, "not even 'the King.' If Kelly could not get his lines untangled, he would be issued a 'no time' and be eliminated from making the finals."

Mark continues, "Dad and I were just having a heck of a time. We did get the horse straightened out — the horse raced and everything went perfect — but that was terrifying. It drove home to me the importance of wagon racing to my dad. I wouldn't say my dad was scared — he'd been in a million similar situations — but I don't think he'd been in one where something that simple could cost him a shot at the Calgary Stampede. I think that idea really bothered him, and probably scared him."

Another year, Mark stood with his dad's wagon just before Calgary's final heat. He vividly remembers, "I got out of the wagon and as I held Dad's leaders, I gave them a little pat on the chest, telling them, 'You gotta do it.' I talked to those horses. Dad went out and won the race, and I felt I had an integral part."

For these latest greenhorns, the treasured childhood memories and games create a bond to the sport, yet devotion is not enough to develop a competent driver. As with Bensmiller, Nevada, and Sutherland, it takes years of handling horses, breaking horses, and working with the lines. Time is needed to learn to appreciate what their horses are thinking through the lines, to develop an understanding of their horses' physical and mental abilities. To gain these talents, these young men still depend upon the tutelage of their fathers, families, and friends.

At age fifteen, Troy Dorchester began driving pony chariots at home. "I was driving the ponies," recounts Troy, "but then I started golfing at my uncle Gordie's golf course and I lost interest in racing. One day I came home and there's a guy with a horse trailer driving out of our yard. I waved. When I got home Dad said, 'If you want to keep golfin', keep golfin', 'cause your horses are gone.' He sold them all on me."

It was only a year later that Troy's interest was rekindled. He states, "My neighbour Chad Harden had an extra chariot outfit at the Ponoka Stampede and he knew I wanted to drive. Chad said, 'We need a driver. If you can get a cart, you can drive.' So I got a chariot and ended up third in the show — my first show!"

The following year Dorchester established his own pony chariot team, and drove them for three years. Then at age eighteen, he started a pony chuckwagon outfit and practised constantly. He says, "I drove lots of 'four up' all spring, and even in the fall when I was done racing."

Troy planned to drive ponies until he could afford a thoroughbred wagon. His dad had retired, but pro driver Jerry Bremner came to him and asked, "If you want to drive a big wagon, I'll give you the horses if you work for me. But you've got to find your own sponsor and wagon." Dorchester said "Sure!" He recalls, "We had a hell of a year [1993]: I finished seventeenth, and Jerry won Calgary and the World."

Dorchester remains grateful for Bremner's bolstering. "It was tough for Jerry to support my outfit, 'cause if a horse got too tired or sore, we shipped him home and we would be short a horse or two. There are a lot of guys who wouldn't give a young guy a chance."

Whereas Dorchester hooked into the pony wagons, Mark Sutherland helped his father and outrode on the pro wagon circuit. By gaining his initial race experience as an outrider, Mark was following in the boot prints of his dad, Bensmiller, and Nevada.

Mark admits, however, that his outriding career was less than illustrious. He describes, "I outrode for about six years. One year I was riding for my uncle Kirk at Calgary. That year, Kirk had an amazing starting outfit. He had a powerhouse of a big wheeler, but had some outriding penalties, and I was the cause of most of them. One time when I was the stove man, the barrel peg man's horse turned and bumped my horse. My horse jumped forward, knocked me down, and stood on me. When the horn went, I was laying on the stove and the horse was laying on me."

He adds, "It was a good thing the horn blew, or I don't think that horse would've moved. I threw that stove as hard as I could, but I was still five feet behind Kirk. As I remember, I was the only outrider that year who had the distinction of missing a stove at the Calgary Stampede. Needless to say, I wasn't a sought-after outrider."

As an outrider, Mark once more encountered the significance his father placed on winning. He recalls, "At Ponoka, I was throwing stove for Dad and a few other guys. Dad made the finals as did George Normand. The fellas riding for George rode for Dad first call. In true competitive spirit, Dad took the best who [were] on the fence at the time — which didn't include me. So Dad dumped me, and I ended up riding for George. I don't remember who won, but we didn't."

Mark's outriding escapades enabled him to become more comfortable amidst the action of a wagon race. But although it lessened the fear, Mark believes outriding is no substitute for real driving experience. Driving around gopher holes in the field does not compare to 20,000 people watching how you handle the lines. Mark explains, "Quite frankly, I believe cowboys learn how to drive, but they don't learn how to race. If you talk to any wagon driver, he'll tell you it's different when you're racing on the track."

Mark adds, "I drove with my dad, Uncle Kirk, and Ralph Vigen — they all trained together — but to really learn how to compete, you must race. You just don't know how to react to those split-second decisions until you've been in that position enough times. That's why most guys won't have much success during their first seven to ten years. You'll have your flashes — I did, Troy did — but most never became a real threat to win until five to seven years of actual racing experience."

Mark and Troy acknowledge the years of driving apprenticeship it has taken to be competitive. As the men have grown and matured, they have relied upon their teachers. The family elders have shared the wagon seats with their sons, imparting values, perceptions, and insights into wagon racing. It is not only the hard skills they have passed on, but also their attitudes and feelings toward the sport.

Troy explains, "Firstly, Dad was very competitive, and I want to be competitive. The first year he ran at Calgary in '67 he made the finals, then he won it in '68. He was tough every time, and I want to be like that too. I don't want to take twenty years to do anything." He continues, "The other thing I learned is to take care of the horses. Ever since I was young I loved looking after the horses, and Dad and Uncle Dallas were always good caretakers. They always had their horses looking good, and I'm hoping I do the same."

Mark also believes there a number of characteristics that he tries to mirror. "It's not just Dad's ability," he emphasizes, "it's his drive, his work ethics, and the way he cares for horses. It's a total package." He adds, "Dad broke the horses, and I either had to attempt to drive with the same style he did, or I would have had more trouble. The thing about wagon racing is that no two guys will drive the same. I suppose it's like hockey — I don't think everyone will skate the same. But I have tried to emulate Dad's technique and winning ways.

"In my opinion, I've got the best wagon driver that's ever raced in my corner, and he's passing down secrets and ideas. I've got an unfair advantage, and I hope it pays off. I'd like to think, certainly one day, that I'm going to come out every night and win day money. If I can be like Dad or Buddy Bensmiller, who year in and year out are a reasonable bet to win day money, I'll be a very happy guy."

The novices' education is one of hands-on practice. They learn about horsemanship, harness repairs, shoeing horses, and veterinary skills; and they spend hours — and years — practising. They turn the barrels at home and race against friends at the local track, but there is always the first race — the first solo trip. Their young dreams finally become a blur of reality. For some greenhorns, it can be more than they expected.

Troy Dorchester admits the one and only time he was ever scared in a wagon was during his first professional race. He recalls, "I was hooked against Reg Johnstone, Gordon 'Spunky' Stewart, and Tyler Helmig. I made a nice barrel turn, and was out there with them guys. We were going into the third and fourth turns and I got all excited. I was on the outside of Reg Johnstone's stove rack, Tyler was right in front of me, and Spunky was right in behind me."

He adds, "I got very excited, 'cause I thought mine were going to come home [first]. So I started bouncing. My feet came off the front of the box and I went out and over the wagon. I went headfirst, but managed to get my hands out to grab the pole. The only things that didn't go out all the way were my legs — they got hooked onto the seat. I got straightened out, crawled back in on the seat, but I only had one line in my hand.

"All the outriders yelled, 'Troy, Troy, are you okay?' 'Yep, I think so,' I shouted." Dorchester managed to grab the rest of his lines and safely finished the race.

He states, "I don't bounce too often any more."

When the rookies enter the track, not only must they worry about their own misadventures, but they also must be wary of their competitors' strategies. The camaraderie found in the barns ends on the track. The rookies enter the domain of the skilful veterans.

The veterans will test the beginners' driving prowess. Mark Sutherland explains, "Some drivers can hold their lines just the right way, directing their horses where they want. One guy in particular held me in on the rail. I was ahead of him and I had every right to move out one or two feet, but I didn't want to hit his horses. He kept his team right next to me, and I lost the race." Mark submits, "It was a mind game. It's not something I'd be confident enough to do myself, but he did, and it paid off for him. I also saw it backfire on him once, but that's the chance he takes."

Dorchester, too, has faced crafty drivers. He describes how at the start of the race, "some of the old guys take their time coming into the barrels. Us young guys want to get in there and go right away, but they come in slow." Troy's uncle Dallas has advised him, "Slow down when you're going into the barrels, 'cause going in fast can screw you up." While the experienced drivers are still easing to the start barrel, the younger drivers are already anxiously waiting, anticipating the horn — as are their horses. Troy says, "If you're sitting waiting and the horn doesn't blow, one horse will make a little move and the other three will think, 'Holy shit, we're outta here.' So you've go to watch some of those drivers that way."

Veterans will also push young drivers wide on the track. Dorchester explains, "Take Kelly [Sutherland]. If he knows you're taking a run at him, he'll take a little more of the racetrack so you've got a longer way to go around. But that's his advantage, he's a tough turning guy. It'd be different if you could get off the barrels ahead of him and give him some of his own medicine. You don't even realize you've been pushed until you watch it on TV and see, 'Holy man, has he got me wide.'"

Kelly Sutherland has a reputation of elbowing rookies and veterans. Around the racetrack's first turn, if Kelly has made the inside rail position but knows the wagon to his right has the ability to pass him, he has been known to drift his wagon out about three feet and snap back. The rear end of his wagon shoots straight sideways, and his challenger is left kissing the outside fence.

Overall though, the rookies feel the older drivers try to help them, especially off the track and in the barns. Cowboys like Buddy and Kelly realize they need capable young drivers to keep the sport entertaining and fresh, and they advise the newcomers.

As a sign of their feelings towards their heroes, young drivers will often uphold traditions their forefathers originated. For example, Dorchester's wagon box is painted with the same distinctive diamond pattern used by his grandfather. Troy also wears a memento of his grandfather in every race. He explains, "I wear my grandpa's old hat for good luck. He won Calgary in '72 with it, and I've worn that hat since I've run ponies. I don't know what I'm going to do if it gets run over and wrecked. I don't let that hat get too far from me when I'm ready to go to the races."

Illustrating his attachment to the hat, he recounts a prank played on him. "Driver Norm Cuthbertson pulled one on me, my first night at Calgary. I was stall-walkin' pretty good, I was so excited. I was tenser than hell. About an hour before the races, I went to grab my hat and it was gone. I thought, 'Oh, my God!' I thought I was going to have a nervous breakdown.

"All of a sudden my hat's back, and I happen to see Norm going out the other end of my barn. So I figured out who it was. I don't know why he'd do it to me — he's the same way, he's got to have a certain hat — but I got him back a month later at the Strathmore show."

Troy emphasizes, "I only wear that hat during wagon season. If I give it six months off each year, maybe it'll give me another ten years."

Rookies are edgy as they head into their first Calgary Stampede, just as Bensmiller, Nevada, and Sutherland were. These young men spent their childhood summers playing in the Stampede barns, and it really is a dream come true to compete in the Rangeland Derby.

Mark recounts, "You never forget your first turn around Calgary's track — for a couple of reasons. Aside from the excitement, the dirt on the racetrack stings your face. It stings like no other dirt can. You don't feel it when you're racing, but you sure do when you're practising in the mornings. It doesn't really clump — there are no rocks — it's just a sand that's different than any other racetrack."

Troy enthusiastically recalls his first Stampede race. "I was going up the track and my uncle Dallas was riding with me. We're going into the barrels and Dallas is giving the big coaching spiel, emphasizing, 'Just make your barrels . . . Just make your barrels . . .' And I'm going, 'Holy shit!' Then Joe Carbury started announcing, 'Back after a two-year delay of the Dorchester name is Troy Dorchester.' People just started screaming, and I got tingles all over when he said my name."

By finally making the cut to race at the Calgary Stampede, the rookies begin to receive the attention once reserved for their elders. The exposure at Calgary pushes the rookies into the forefront of the chuckwagon world. No longer are they just the heir, or the student, but they are now drivers in their own right.

This new position can sometimes create unexpected pressures from family and fans. In the instances of Sutherland and Dorchester, their family names are linked to chuckwagon dynasties. This recognition assists in terms of earning more lucrative sponsorship, but it can also lead to false expectations. Some fans assume, and expect, that the rookies will succeed as notably as their namesakes.

Mark Sutherland responds, "I suppose in my case, some people unrealistically think that there is going to be another Kelly Sutherland. In case they haven't noticed, there isn't. There might be, but there isn't right now. Guys who have had very competitive careers, like Troy's uncle Dallas, left on their own terms, and they didn't win half as much as Dad." He adds, "I would love to match everything Dad did, but realistically, I don't think it's going to happen." He laughs, "I'd like to win half as much, and I still might be the second-most-winning driver in history. So that wouldn't be too bad."

Mark feels the most important pressure he faces is self-imposed. He knows his own limits. "I don't expect to win the World title eight times. I do expect to get my fair share, but in all reality my fair would be one, maybe two times. You say three times, and you say guys are dominating decades."

Mark pulls no punches when he says, "I don't feel I'm setting my standards too low to say I probably won't win or dominate like my dad. In a way I wish I was, or hope I was, or hope I will be, but in a way I don't. I liken it to how I expect what Gretzky felt when he was eclipsing his hero Gordie Howe. I just don't know how I'd feel about that. But like I said, I don't think it's an issue I'm going to have to deal with."

Dorchester is also grateful his family has not placed undue pressure on him. Troy says, "I don't think my dad or my other uncles have any expectations. Dad and Uncle Dallas come to quite a few of the shows, and let me know about the horses. It's sometimes hard for me to tell which horse is starting hard and which one isn't turning. They tell me, 'Well that pig, he ain't starting.' Plus they always pass on confidence back at the barn, saying, 'Good job,' 'Nice turn.' Just that alone helps."

Troy adds, "I've got sponsorships the last few years because of my last name, and not because of what I had done." At the 2000 Calgary Stampede canvas auction, Troy Dorchester's tarp sold for $85,000, and Mark Sutherland's sold for $62,000. Troy says, "You've got guys like Jim Nevada — he's a worker, but it's still taken him a while to finally get the sponsorship he deserves."

Dorchester feels his good fortune has not affected his friendships. "My friends always gave me a hard time, joking that I got the sponsorship because of my name, but after winning two shows in '99, I showed that I am a good driver." And his positive nature is reflected in how he deals with the ribbing and competitiveness. "For me, no matter what people say, I just enjoy travelling in the summer. One night you might have hard feelings against a guy over a race, and the next morning you can go down and have coffee with him. It's over. It's done with."

In a sport with tight rivalries, these rookies do not feel their family names have prejudiced their peers. They, and not their names, must speak for themselves. Mark Sutherland jokes, "Well, I suppose if they can't beat 'the King,' the next best thing is to throw a little mud in my face; but in reality the drivers probably approach me the same way they approach anyone else they race against. I'm just a competitor out there when the horn goes."

Nevertheless, Mark realizes there is one cowboy on the racetrack who brings a special aspect to competition: his father, his hero. This makes for a complex relationship. Unlike Troy Dorchester, whose father retired before they could race together, Mark must defeat his father if he is to win. For Mark, it is an arduous route to victory.

He explains, "At the '99 Ponoka Stampede I almost realized a lifelong dream of making the finals — the Dash for Cash — against my dad. Unfortunately, Ponoka only takes three wagons and I was fourth; but if I'm going to be competitive, I am going to be racing against him."

Mark feels a dream come true would be he and his father competing in the Calgary Stampede finals, as Tommy Glass and his son Jason did in 1997. Mark says, "I talked to Tommy about racing together, and I talked to Jason about it, and in all reality, I think it was better for Tommy, judging by the glimmer in their eyes."

Mark adds, "The unfortunate part about father-and-son wagon drivers is that Tommy was on top of the sport, and Jason was down on bottom, and at some point they were going to meet in the middle. Jason will have to defeat his father. For Jason to achieve his dream, he has to squash his hero's dream. I suppose that's maybe why the gleam in Tommy's eye was a little brighter because he'd already done what he wanted to do in the sport, and was pleased Jason was racing against him. Maybe Jason knew it was near the end for Tommy's career." Tom Glass retired in 1999.

Kelly Sutherland has told his son that he would love to see them both racing in the Calgary Stampede final. Mark shares, "I know he'd treat me like any other competitor, but I bet he'd be cheering for me. I just want to be competitive, and to be a legitimate contender while Dad's still there to race against. I want to say if I won the Calgary Stampede, that I beat the best, when he was there, when he was competitive."

It is not easy emotionally for wagon drivers to defeat their heroes. All wagon drivers are competitive, no matter whom they are hitched up against. And although it is perceived as a reckless, callous sport, chuckwagon racing and its rookies have their firm basis in the goodwill of family. Already these cowboys are reflecting upon how important their fathers have been to their careers. This deep respect binds youth to the sport and is transferred to succeeding generations.

As for their prospects, Troy and Mark are optimistic and energetic. Mark says, "I see a great future for wagon racing, and I see myself in that future." They are eager to display their horsemanship, to prove themselves, and to win. In 1999, Troy

Dorchester finished second to Kelly Sutherland in the Calgary Stampede final, and in 2000 he again made the final four. The young drivers' time is coming.

Despite their ambitions, these young wagon drivers do have moments when they question their chosen career. Troy Dorchester, a passionate horseman, second-guesses himself when he deals horses. "I start wondering, 'Should I sell this horse? Is it going to hurt me next year? Am I going to be kicking myself in the butt if I see these horses running by me in the racetrack?'" He also recognizes, "I get too close to my horses — my dad even tells me that — 'cause I hate selling them. Once you've had a horse, it's hard to let them go. All mine end up like being a little kid's pony; I fall for them too easily."

Troy adds, "When I do sell a horse, in the back of my mind, I think, 'Gawd, I shouldn't have made that change,' but you always need youth. You've always got to make room for new ones. I haven't had an instance where I've felt I shouldn't have sold a horse yet, but it's probably coming."

It's obvious Dorchester's heart is with his horses. He sincerely loves working with, talking about, and watching them. "One of the toughest times is losing a horse," he states. "When I retire a horse, I leave them in the pasture until they get so bad that they can't eat, or their teeth are bad, or whatever. Then I'll put them down." Troy has already started a burial yard. "It's kind of a sad thing. In 1999, I lost a good outriding horse when he broke his back at home. Somehow he either hit a tree or rolled funny. I only had three horses that I started with in '93, and he was one of them, so it was pretty tough. But now he's got his little spot here; like I said, I get pretty attached to them.

"You have horses for a long time, and I think they need to be remembered," he adds. "Losing a horse is not something us drivers bring up, because it's something we hate."

For Mark Sutherland, his doubts surface off the track, when he reflects upon his playmates' achievements. "For me, I see my friends succeeding, like Jason Glass and Troy, and although these guys have at least five years more experience than I do, it's tough. But I've also made other things more important than wagon racing, like family. It's tough to make wagon racing your number one focus, when it really isn't — family is."

Sutherland's work as a schoolteacher has perhaps interfered with his consistency. Mark made the cut for the Calgary Stampede in 1996 and 2000. The two years prior, 1995 and 1999, were the only two seasons when Mark did not teach. Based on this pattern, he has decided to put his teaching career on hold in order to succeed in the wagons.

Conceding their apprehensions, these animated men remain enthusiastic about the next year and focused on their ambitions. Chuckwagon driving is what they were bred, taught, and even called to do. Within these rookies, the blood of wagon racing gallops fiercely. Their eyes glimmer with the hope of the ensuing season, the possibilities of victories, and the laughter to be shared with friends. They are living their dreams, and the dreams of their heroes.

Dorchester emphasizes he finds participating in the sport entirely rewarding. He says, "You feel pretty good when you can get an outfit all joined up, and go out and run tough. It's kind of like any kind of sporting team: if you get 'em all lined up right, you're going to win some big games, making the coach feel pretty good — and I'm the coach. This is my National Hockey League. I'm living a lifelong dream; this is totally fulfilling for me."

Sutherland adds, "I continue to love the feeling after you've turned the top barrel, the horses hang a left at the bottom barrel and head into the first turn. The power that you feel is just amazing. The horses are all charging. It almost feels like the front of the wagon jumps every time they grab another step. It's exhilarating."

Mark explains what rookies strive for. "I still remember very vividly the first time I outran anybody who was one of the great ones. During the Ponoka Stampede, in '93 or '94, I was on Barrel 1, and Troy's uncle Dallas was on Barrel 2. As usual it was a 'black hole' in Ponoka. Fifteen feet from the rail it was absolute muck — mud and water. If you had one wheel in it, you were slow.

"I raced on the inside rail and Dallas went easy on me, never putting me down in that mud. He let me run. Maybe he thought of coming in, but Dallas knew it might not have been safe, and maybe he just looked at my smile and thought, 'Maybe we'll let this kid go.' I outran him and I thought I'd won the Calgary Stampede."

Mark adds, "The next two years were great, and I regularly raced against Tommy Glass. At one point he was sitting first in the World and I was sitting second. Guys were concerned, 'Gosh, am I going to be hooked with Mark? He's going to out-turn me, and he's going to outrun me, and I'm not going to have an easy go of it.' That was the greatest feeling I've ever had, and what I've always wanted — guys to be planning their strategy around me — not me planning around them."

Looking toward the clock, Mark suggests, "To dominate the sport like Dad did, or even be competitive like Dad, I've got to start pretty quickly. I'm almost thirty years old — ten years away from forty. Maybe next year. That's the beauty of the sport."

One day Troy Dorchester and Mark Sutherland will savour the adulation once reserved for their predecessors. They remain pledged to the sport's generations, and they urge the sport with assured, capable hands. Already, these men are admired and imitated by children playing chuckwagon in the barns. "Hyaw! I'm Troy Dorchester . . . Hyaw! I'm Mark Sutherland," the boys' yells ring out. Their youthful shouts echo through the stalls, past the shadows of teamsters long gone. The Chuckwagon cowboy genesis continues.

CHAPTER 9

Aiming Their Poles

The last specialist I saw told me I should stop acting like Hulk Hogan, when I was built like Pee-wee Herman. When I was younger I didn't have the muscle mass, so I did a lot on adrenaline. My shoulders are both worn out, I've only got one eye that works, I'm missing some teeth, and I have a few health problems from landing on my head too many times . . . but I'm not where I want to be yet.

JIM NEVADA

With the arrival of vigorous, brazen competitors, chuckwagon racing is wheeling on to new ranges. Bensmiller, Nevada, and Sutherland are the navigators, steering the sport's newcomers. With Sutherland's impulsive experience, Bensmiller's horse sense, and Nevada's fervour, these men are charting an ambitious course for the wagons, for their sons, and for themselves. Similar to the trail bosses of the continental cattle drives, they are riding point, guiding chuckwagon racing's future.

Leading the wagon herd, Bensmiller and Sutherland feel their greatest legacy will be their sons' participation. Their sons will sustain the sport; and through their sons they will be remembered.

Kelly Sutherland has keenly followed his son's development in wagon racing. With his discerning eye, he has watched Mark both prevail and falter. He emphasizes, "Mark has the necessary soft hands to race." But he adds, "Mark started well when he began, and that traditionally can happen. The first year or two, guys have a real good Cinderella year, and then they kind of go into the tank and start second-guessing themselves."

Sutherland is convinced Mark has turned a vital corner. Kelly says, "I think Mark will get tough from now on. He bought his own livestock and is travelling on his own. If he wants to be a wagon driver, then I want him to be tough enough to do it for a living, which means he's got to qualify for Calgary. He'll determine where he ends up on the totem pole just by how much he sacrifices and how determined he is. He'll learn that to win a bunch does not come easy."

Kelly recognizes today's newcomers do not enjoy the advantages he benefitted from. "I started in a time of major transition. There were only sixteen drivers; now there are up to fifty. I had so much experience by the time I was twenty-five. Mark will be thirty-five by the time he has the same experience." He expands, "Since there were fewer drivers, we drove two outfits every night. I always had one outfit that was "really good," and one that was "fairly good." The "fairly good" team always went first each night, and I could experiment how to set my lines. Today's young guys don't have that opportunity, and that's their disadvantage to achieve what I have achieved in the sport."

Sutherland emphasizes, "I try not to say too much to Mark, because I find myself being quite critical of the way he drives and the way he holds the horses. Sometimes I can sense the horse wants to work, but he won't let him work. He doesn't know he's not letting him work, and it's so hard to tell him." He describes, "The horse wants to start, wants to charge, but with the way he's got the lines, the horse can't. The horse is getting the wrong signals. I try to tell him, and he finds that really frustrating. But I was like that too when Ralph Vigen was trying to teach me."

Kelly considers, "To me, Mark doesn't seem to be driven enough, but his friend Jason Glass says Mark would do anything to win, anything. Mark portrays a different air to other people than he does to me."

Twenty-nine-year-old Jason Glass and the rising generation are setting their sights on the veterans, especially Kelly Sutherland. Sutherland smiles, "Jason Glass wants to win in the worst way, but it just so happens I happen to be in the middle of the road. I don't think he hates me, but he sure as hell wishes I'd go away. When he does beat me, I always go over and shake his hand. At some point I'm going to make a mistake — my luck's going to run out — and something's going to happen. That's just the way it works. There's no doubt Jason is going to be World champion."

Sutherland shares, "I feel the younger guys kind of think I'm weird. They look at me, they realize the amount of driving passion I have, and they try to figure out how to get it."

Buddy Bensmiller's seventeen-year-old son, Kurt, shares the same wagon fever that gripped Kelly Sutherland, Jim Nevada, and Buddy. "Wagons are all Kurt talks about," says Buddy. "It's all he wants to do. I don't know what puts it into him. Kurt doesn't like riding the horses, but as soon as he picks up a set of lines, it's different."

Buddy is doing all he can to assist Kurt. He plans to haul Kurt's horses and wagon on the WPCA tour, enabling Kurt to begin his driving career while he finishes Grade 11. Buddy says, "I'm going to have to pack him. There's no way he can afford to start. I don't know how a young guy can afford to start on his own. Maybe I've built up something, so that if he goes out and has a decent year, and he's a good, polite kid, maybe some sponsor will notice him and spend their money on him."

Bensmiller adds, "Now Kurt just needs experience, lots of experience. I figured if he's going to start, he'll have two years to get experience, and when he's out of school he should be good enough to run at Calgary. He can start making a living from wagons."

Presently, Bensmiller feels wagon racing lacks "celebrity" drivers. It takes several years for fans to relate to, and cheer for, new faces. He says, "In the late '90s, we lost some of our veterans. We need some "name" drivers, and I think Kurt's last name should help him out. Time will tell, I guess."

Kelly Sutherland believes the present strength of the sport bodes well for the newcomers like Kurt. He remarks, "When I started, if someone would've told me my son would be able to get $100,000 in sponsorship, I would have laughed at him. That's happened for three or four young guys, because the older stars are leaving. Some of the guys are blessed with the right last name, and as long as they are competitive they'll be able to make a lot of money from the sport."

In contrast, Jim Nevada hopes his young son, Will, pursues a more sensible sport — something other than wagon racing. "I'd prefer my son was good with a golf club or a hockey stick, rather than a chuckwagon horse. In golfing, all you need is a caddy, but in wagons you need a semi, a gooseneck RV trailer, a wagon trailer, and a farm." Nevada adds, "I just can't see why a kid or anyone with half a brain would start off being a wagon driver nowadays, unless a sponsor helped. It's a big investment with no guarantees."

He notes, however, "Will is the last Nevada left, the only one to carry on the Nevada name, and I'll support him in whatever he wants to do." Nevada is committed to standing behind his son, even if Will grows up to be a cowboy. Nevada states, "If he does decide to be a wagon driver, I will tell him, 'You've got to be a good horseman. You've got to understand your horses and give them proper care, to the best of your abilities.'"

As youthful drivers replace the veterans, Jim Nevada feels the sport is changing for the better. The recruits seem to place a higher emphasis on sportsmanship. "I like the younger crowd," says Nevada. "Years ago it was rough and rowdier. Some of the old guys were just jerks — they'd run you tight, and play all kind of games. If you got into a 'hole' on the track, you'd have trouble, and your competitors might leave you in there. Your arms got so tired that you couldn't feel your harness; you might pile your outfit up.

"Nowadays everybody gives each other room. There are a few idiots like in any sport, but it's fun again. Ninety-nine percent of us like each other and get along great — there's the odd asshole, but you can't get away from that."

And in his barn, too, Nevada is grateful for the fellowship. He is especially thankful for his barn crew's assistance, and even their advice. Nevada says, "With my crew, they all give their suggestions and their two cents' worth, but the final call is always me. I've got the money out, it's my investment, and that's the way it should be. I'll listen to them and make my decision. Sometimes they'll come up to me and say, 'I told you so.' I live and learn."

One of the dilemmas faced by the cowboys is how to broaden the backing for the sport. Chuckwagon racing is an incongruous activity in the increasingly urban landscape. The sport thrives on its rural roots, and people who have no ties to the land or to raising animals often have difficulty appreciating the sport. The image of chuckwagons poses a complex challenge.

Often the cowboys are wrangling against the changing expectations of the "New West." The new urban society seeks out the myth of the cowboy, through art, entertainment, and music, but the reality of ranching and cowboy life is misunderstood. The cowboys are horse lovers in an automobile age. The people in rural towns continue their support, but that populace is changing. And more and more, the chuckwagons' future relies upon the urban population.

Jim Nevada has encountered the problems of urban perceptions in his local community. Airdrie is a rural-based city, but it has become a commuter community for Calgary. He remarks, "The local Airdrie newspaper does not stand behind us wagon drivers. Driver Ron David retired and they had nothing written about him. The paper doesn't follow us for the whole season. Kids at the wading pool get more pictures in the paper than we do."

Nevada adds, "The older Airdrie crowd still comes to talk to me all the time, but this is a young town, and the people live here because it's cheap, and it's easy to commute to Calgary. Other than living here, they have nothing to do with Airdrie. There have been some great cowboys and cowgirls that have come out of Airdrie, but as of support from this town, it sucks. That's a sore spot with me."

At the racetracks, Nevada observes another disturbing trend. Looking into the grandstands at shows outside of Calgary, he notices, "They're filled with grey hairs." Nevada is concerned that wagon racing is not appealing to a younger audience and feels the sport needs to re-emphasize its youthfulness, especially with so many fresh drivers now competing. Otherwise, the fan base may simply die away.

On the other hand, Kelly Sutherland believes the profile of the sport in Western Canada is very high. Yet he is also aware that the public has a mistaken picture of how much money chuckwagon cowboys make from the sport. The perception is that the cowboys' wallets, especially Kelly's, are lined with bills. Fans do not appreciate the escalating expenses of maintaining horses.

Sutherland says, "People read the headlines that my canvas sells to a sponsor for $165,000, but they don't realize I spend at least $100,000 maintaining the operation that I run. That amount includes wages, repairs, and maintenance. To upgrade my investment is over and above that amount. Plus, I sell my weak stock at fifty cents and buy replacement stock at a dollar."

When Bensmiller visits Sutherland, he always pokes fun at Kelly's success with sponsors. Inside Kelly's barn, old wagon tarps hang on the walls, and Buddy asks him, "How many of those companies are still going?" to which Kelly answers, "None, they're all broke." Bensmiller laughs, "The sponsors Kelly has had, they all end up going broke." But Buddy adds, "Kelly's been great for the sport. He's a pain in the ass sometimes, but he's got the sponsorship to where it is."

To widen the sport's appeal, and to increase the incomes of those drivers whose costs exceed their earnings, the cowboys are looking to new ideas. One proposal has been to extend the wagon season. However, wagon racing is limited by the horsepower — literally. Their engines only have so much "run." Sutherland states, "We can only race till the end of August. By the time September comes around, those horses are finished. If you continue to run them, you're going to hurt them." Nevada agrees, "We have forty-two racing dates now and the younger guys can't afford the kind of horsepower needed to do any more days. By the end of the season their horses are just spent. If the horses are not rested, they still do the job, but they don't perform to their peak. They're just like a human, and they need rest or they don't work as hard."

Nevada adds, "If you blast the horses every weekend without giving them a break, by the end of the season you've got nothing. You're there just to fill a heat up. I've been there. The guys at the bottom aren't making any money as it is, so we shouldn't make the season longer and torture them more." He also notes, "Most guys work one or two jobs all winter so they can race all summer and lose money. They're not a Kelly Sutherland who has sixty horses at home; they are Joe Kid, who has ten to twelve at most. Kelly's alright, his son Mark's alright — he's part of the lucky sperm group. New kids starting out are toast."

Rather than extending the summer circuit to augment incomes, the cowboys have alternatively proposed running a separate United States tour during the winter months. However, wagon racing has never fully captured the American imagination.

For a country epitomized by the idea of the Wild West, wagon racing has yet to gain sweeping public interest.

As an experiment into the southern U.S. market, in 1996 the wagons appeared for three days at Pomona, California. Jim Nevada recalls, "We were advertised as the 'Crazy Canucks.' The people there had a tough time realizing wagon racing is a pro sport — it's competitive, and there's a lot of money. They didn't realize it's so aggressive."

He continues, "Until they saw a race they couldn't understand it. They thought we'd pull up in our little stock trailers; but instead we drove up in our semis, parked, and unfolded the barns. Then we brought the horses out, shiny and taken care of; then the chromed harnesses; and then the painted wagons. For the people in California, it was, 'Holy, there is something to this sport. It's not an old wide-wheeled wagon with barrels tied onto the side. It ain't a prairie schooner.'"

To entertain crowds in California, or anywhere south of the Canadian border, long-distance transportation remains a significant hurdle. Kelly Sutherland says, "We need fifty liner loads of horses and equipment to put on a show. It is a very difficult sport to pick up and move. There is a huge cost. That is why we are an Alberta-based sport; everyone lives within two hundred miles of Calgary."

A further impediment is that television is not a viable option for kindling spectators' initial interest or curiosity. The complexity of each race does not fit on a television screen. There is simply too much action. When chuckwagon races have been aired, the races have not attracted the necessary viewership. And in today's multimedia world, the sport's commercial value is limited by its lack of television or Internet revenue.

For most first-time spectators, chuckwagon racing must be seen to be understood. Sutherland says, "I've discovered, if you're just going to put chuckwagon racing on in a new market, and you're going to charge ten dollars, you aren't going to attract enough people to roast a wiener. They don't know what the hell they're buying. They have no idea. I know we can sell it anywhere, but we need a Ted Turner personality, [someone] prepared to put three million dollars into promotions and take the sport on."

Sutherland has always been a firm believer that the sport can be taken into the United States, and he pushed for the races to be hosted in Washington State and California. Sutherland, like visionaries Richard Cosgrave and George Normand, believes there is potential to race year-round. However, when Normand and Cosgrave were killed, the momentum to push south was stalled.

The changing pulse of the drivers' initiatives to race in the U.S., the high transportation costs, and the absence of television revenue are not the only barriers wagon racing faces. There are other obstacles. For example, most of the U.S. racetracks are a lengthy one mile long and they do not have infields. Secondly, in contrast to staging a rodeo, where a promoter essentially needs only corral fencing, bucking chutes, and bucking stock, putting on a chuckwagon race requires a carefully sloped and maintained track. The track is an intimidating cost for fair and exhibition committees.

Also, there is no gambling or parimutuel betting on chuckwagon races, which limits promoters' interest. And finally, there are only a few American cowboys racing pro wagons, especially ones who can win. "We won't be highly successful in the U.S. until we have some American participants winning," says Sutherland. "Once they get a taste of winning, people will become hungry for it."

Buddy Bensmiller comments, "Kelly's got a big speech on where this sport's going, but as far as I'm concerned he's dreaming. Until we can get it to where everyone is making a decent living, the sport can't expand. They're starving to death now, a lot of them guys. The bottom money paid out has to come up."

Bensmiller adds, "Myself, I don't know why the sport hasn't caught on in the States." He suggests, "I guess it is the wrong time of the year. We can't race down there in the summertime, so we have to race in the fall or winter, and most of the rodeos are indoors. Once October rolls around, Americans think it's winter, no matter how cold it is."

In Canada, meanwhile, Buddy believes the sport will endure. But he is concerned about the attitude of the new drivers taking over the sport. He says, "What the hell does the younger generation do? I think the western is getting lost out of our sport. Very few of them have chores, they don't do anything, and they wonder why they're broke. You've got to think down the road. Maybe they can get by on what they're making right now, but someday when they have a family, that extra few thousand dollars from cattle, or whatever, will be worth something when they need it."

Bensmiller is also dismayed by how little other drivers are willing to talk up and promote the sport. "The cowboys think we've got something that people need, but people don't need it. There's more entertainment in this goddam world than anybody needs. We have a hell of a sport that we should be selling to people, but you have to sell it to them." Bensmiller appreciates it is the cowboys themselves who can best move and build the sport.

For the chuckwagon cowboys, the public's misconceptions about the sport and the high financial demands to keep their operations running can be daunting. Wagon racing is expensive, and Jim Nevada feels the monetary costs, combined with activists' pressures, are going to be the demise of the sport. He anticipates the urban-based lobby groups will shut down wagon racing before his son is old enough to possibly compete.

Nevada feels people have forgotten the agrarian connection to life and death. He says, "Most people just don't realize what a rural lifestyle is like. People don't understand they knock runt pigs on their heads because they're going to starve to death. It puts them out of their misery. You do that in front of some city person and they're going to freak. People don't understand that shit."

He adds, "I'd just like to show the tree huggers my horses Pronto or Mister Kerr, both who would've been on a table in France a long time ago if it wasn't for chuckwagon racing. Now they're eating their second cut of an alfalfa bale, worth seventy-five dollars a bale. The unlucky horses don't go to a trail ride in Banff — they're hanging by their hooves in a slaughter plant. That's life."

Sutherland hopes the sport does not become railroaded by the animal-rights lobby, or by safety issues. Amongst the safety proposals under discussion, one suggestion has been to take away the starting figure-eight turn and make the race simply a straight race. Sutherland retorts, "There's definitely an element of danger in the sport. I think that's the only thing that makes it appealing. We made a lot of great changes for safety's sake, but there's only so far you can go without changing the actual sport. We're a spectator sport. If we take anything away from that, so it's not exciting, then we'll lose a lot of the fan base."

Despite the suggestions to change the races, Buddy Bensmiller does not believe wagon racing will be stopped. Nevertheless, he does feel that wrecks and negative publicity have dissuaded the multimillion-dollar sponsorships. He says, "I think it's keeping the big, big money away. Myself, I can't see the sport growing any larger than it is, but I could never see it growing as big as it has, especially for me."

The sport continues to astonish Bensmiller. "If somebody would've told me thirty years ago that if I kept it up and done well at it, I'd make this kind of money, I'd figure he was smoking a joint. I'd never have believed it. We need the money to operate, but that's not why I do it. Not then, and not now."

Nor is money what inspires Kelly Sutherland to keep racing. He says, "Guys are getting sick and tired of me winning. I'm the most hated guy on a wagon now — respected, but hated. It doesn't bother me, 'cause there were a few guys like that when I started.

"I always wanted respect, and as long as you were a competitor, even if you were loved or hated, as long as you were respected, that's what is important. I think I've gained that respect; I've tried to contribute to make the sport that much better for everybody."

After thirty-five seasons, Sutherland still finds wagon racing wonderfully challenging. He states, "Every time you have somebody who dominates the sport consistently, the level of competition rises as drivers try to beat him, which is really good for the sport. I guarantee you, my odds of staying ahead are a lot worse than my competitors' odds of passing me. Nothing beats the old but the young."

As they wink to their pursuing competitors, Sutherland, Nevada, and Bensmiller each have goals still to realize. Looking ahead, Buddy Bensmiller has no interest in retiring from wagon racing. He plans to race as long as his health holds out. He states, "I can't stand not being able to be in the sport. I'd like to go till I was sixty anyway. If the sport's going to be big, it'll be big then. Right now, I make too much money to shut 'er down, and once the kids are on their own, I won't have to rotate as many dollars. I can go back to strictly dealing horses again."

Interestingly, Bensmiller has no desire to be a chuckwagon spectator. "If my kids don't do it, and if I ever quit, I don't know if I'd ever go watch a wagon race. I don't really enjoy watching wagon races. Same thing with a hockey game on television — I'd rather participate. I watch the races at a show, but that's basically to see how the other horses are working, and where the holes are, and where the heavy and hard spots are on the track."

When Bensmiller does retire, one thing he could do is further his skills in water witching. Recently, Buddy watched his neighbour spend $20,000 on trying to find a water source, with no luck. Buddy told him he could witch for water. His neighbour, who had nothing more to lose, said, "Sure, Buddy."

Bensmiller relates, "I used a crowbar as a divining rod. Some people believe in it, and some people don't. The old guys say, 'Go to the highest spot to find water,' and that's what I did." Bensmiller went to the top of the nearby hill. "I just walked around and the crowbar nearly pulled itself out of my hands. I don't know what the force is, but there was a lot of pull." They dug ten feet, and his grateful neighbour found water.

Throughout helping neighbours, working with his cattle, or tutoring his children, Bensmiller's career as a horseman has been paramount. Like his father, he has made a living from his horses. And Bensmiller hopes the family love for horses is carried on. If his sons and daughter continue to work with horses, he will know his wagon career meant something. To Buddy, this bequest is more important than a name in a chuckwagon almanac.

Bensmiller says, "I don't need to be remembered. I ain't done nothing special, I've just been one of the lucky ones."

No matter how prominent their accomplishments may be, Jim Nevada is skeptical that chuckwagon drivers leave indelible memories. He shares, "I'm weird, I guess, I just don't think anyone is going to remember a chuckwagon driver fifty years down the line unless they look in a record book. If they do, I'd like to be remembered as a fair driver and a competitive one, not a loser. Maybe I'm just getting old and owly, but I don't think anyone else remembers."

Nevada foresees an extended career driving; however, he feels pulled toward other adventures. He and Kim have made travelling the world a priority, taking such trips as sailing and scuba diving around the British Virgin Islands. Jim says, "I'd like to take a couple of years off and go travelling, before our son, Will, gets into school. There are a couple places in the world I'd like to go see. It is a very realistic possibility."

He adds, "I would like another five to ten years of racing. I don't see myself driving till I'm sixty-five. I like the sport, but there are other things I want to do while I'm still young enough to do them. I'm thirty-five now, and my doctor says I've got the body of a fifty-year-old."

Ignoring his aches and pains, though, Nevada is determined not to "stove up" until he realizes his personal goals. Each season he becomes a fiercer, more capable driver. The Calgary Stampede and the World championship become less elusive each year. Nevada will pursue his ambitions until he prevails. Nevada states, "I'm not a quitter." He stresses, "Everything I do, I'm really driven. I'm really competitive. If somebody tells me I can't do it, I'll do it just to prove to them that I can. I will do it till I get it right, or to where I want to go with it.

"I want to be in the record books, so when it says 'Calgary Stampede Champion 2002,' it says 'Jim Nevada.' When I retire I can see my name there. I don't want to retire and never have made it there. In any sport I've tried, I've always finished what I started. I've always been a winner."

Approaching his fiftieth year, Sutherland is indebted to wagon racing. He stresses, "Everything I have basically revolves around chuckwagon racing. It wasn't that way for my family before, but it's been that way for me. It has opened so many doors for me in my life. Even when I went to find the best cancer doctors for my dad, people recognized me and helped us."

He adds, "Hopefully we can get to the same financial rewards of other pro sports. If my son stays in it, I'd like to see him make a living just off of wagon racing. Man, that'd be the life to live, guaranteed. I think the sport is just so healthy now. We've got a very, very good start in the twenty-first century. Hopefully I'm around to be a part of it for a while."

Kelly Sutherland has now reached the point in his career when he can assess how he wants to leave the sport. He states, "My last few years, I want to propel the sport to a level as high as I can take it, and hopefully there's someone else [who] will come along and keep pushing." Kelly adds, "We have a huge advantage over rodeo events, since our competitors have such long careers in the sport. Therefore, you can build huge star systems. We have sports stars; it's just a matter of convincing people they are stars."

Nevertheless, even a chuckwagon cowboy's star loses its lustre. Eventually, the "toughness" characterizing the superlative cowboys wanes. Sutherland shares, "Ralph Vigen won the Calgary Stampede at age sixty-two, so that gives you an idea of how long a cowboy can last. I don't think I'll last that long. The sport's changed so much since then; it's more competitive, there's more pressure, and as you get older you can't stand that pressure."

He adds, "Most people in their fifties, they quit being competitive, they quit taking that chance. If you don't take that chance, you ain't going to win. That's not to say they quit driving — they just lost something they had before."

Sutherland believes he will know when he has lost the nerve to keep taking the necessary chances. When he does, he will quit. "I'll try to stay involved in the sport, helping out my son, and maybe promoting the wagons full-time. There's probably going to be room for a drivers' agent. Certain corporations want certain drivers, but sometimes the wrong sponsor gets hooked up with the wrong individual. There's room for somebody to play a role."

Once his harness is hung up for good, Sutherland wants to be remembered for two things. "Number one, for the fierce competitor I am. Number two, for being able to contribute greatly to the sport." He adds, "I hope people don't think I just wanted to take from the sport all the time, which people do [think] when you win a lot. Chuckwagon racing is bigger than any one man, and sometime, this sport is going to be more financially rewarding for a lot of people. I hope some of the things that got it there can be attributed to me, that's all."

He concludes, "I can see an end to my career, but I still want to put enough marks on that wall so that they don't forget who it was who put them there."

Chuckwagon cowboys have entrenched themselves in the western landscape. They are real-life heroes, nurturing the passion of the sport's trailblazers. Their community keeps alive a distinctive lifestyle, sharing joy and tears. Chuckwagon cowboys are part of western legends, and they bring to mind a fabled time — when the range was open and free, and cowboys were as good as their horses.

The character of the romantic West lives on in the small town of High River, Alberta. Surrounded by ranches, cattle, and horses, it is the centre of Alberta's ranching country. In the nearby foothills, toward the Rocky Mountains, Guy Weadick, the founder of chuckwagon racing, owned his Stampede Ranch. Today, Weadick lies buried in High River's cemetery. In this ranching town, the spirit of chuckwagon racing rests secure.

Each June in High River, the chuckwagon cowboys gather to race. Often as their races end, a spectacular sunset shades the darkening "big sky" with flaring vermilion and ochre hues. With the sun descending behind the silhouetted mountains, the tired horses whinny contentedly to one another. And around the racetrack, corralled by the trucks and motorhomes, the chuckwagon fans, sponsors, and families relax amidst the horse stalls. Grandparents, parents, and children are playing, socializing, and sharing stories — their cheerful laughter rises above the sanctuary of the circled wagons.

This is the frontier warmth of chuckwagon racing.

As the sky deepens from violet to black, Bensmiller, Nevada, and Sutherland prepare to turn in for the night. Having checked on their horses, the cowboys head wearily to their trailers. Walking through the dirt and mud, they plot the next evening's races. The men are also planning for their sons — vigilant to their growth, moulding the sport's destiny.

Finally, there is one last chore. In keeping with a tradition that harks back to the teamsters of the open range, the cowboys look for the North Star, their guiding star. They turn their wagon poles — and their hopes and dreams — to its course. They are setting their course for the future. Tomorrow, the wagons will roll.

The chuckwagon spirit runs on.

GLOSSARY

Barrel: Two barrels distinguish each figure-eight pattern. Initially, actual wooden barrels were used; now they are manufactured from a flexible plastic that can be moulded and reshaped.

Barrel peg: The tent peg situated at the left side of the wagon, closest to the barrel at the race's start.

Barrel peg man: The outrider who has the job of throwing in the barrel peg.

Bridle: Part of the tack or harness that secures a bit in the horse's mouth.

Canvas, or tarp: The material covering the bows on the rear box of the wagon. The canvas carries the name of the wagon's driver and the sponsor.

Chalk line: Temporary chalk lines drawn in the infield dirt to delineate wagon lanes.

Chuckbox: A pantry-like box built at the back of a range "chuck wagon." It held all a camp cook would need to feed the working cowboys, including cast-iron kettles, Dutch ovens, food, cutlery, and the coffee pot.

Cooper: Someone who builds or repairs barrels.

Cow-pie: A flat, round piece of cow dung.

Cowpuncher: A synonym for cowboy. Also cowhand, cowpoke, and cowprod.

Day money: The prize money awarded to the outfit with the fastest time for one evening's races.

Doubletree: A pivoted three-foot-long bar, bolted to the wagon pole. A singletree is attached to either end of the doubletree.

Draw pin: The pin holding the wagon pole to the wagon.

Eatin' irons: Silverware or cutlery.

Four up: Four horses.

Grub slinger: Chuckwagon cook.

Hame: Either one of two J-shaped pieces lying on either side of the collar in a horse's harness, to which the traces or tugs are fastened.

Hame strap: A strap connecting the two hames.

Hand: A unit of length equal to four inches, used to measure a horse's height from the ground to the top of the horse's withers.

Leader: One of the front pair of the four-horse team.

Lines: Long leather straps connected to the horse's bridle by dividing leather straps (crosschecks). The lines are the primary tool the chuckwagon drivers use to control their horses.

Long barrel: Barrel 1. It is the inside starting barrel position. On the long barrel, the distance between the two barrels making up the figure-eight turn is the greatest.

Northern Chuckwagon Association: Name used by wagon drivers situated in northern Saskatchewan, Manitoba, and northeastern Alberta. In 1979 the association changed its name to the Northern Professional Chuckwagon Association, and in 1995 it became the Canadian Professional Chuckwagon Association.

Off-barrel peg: The tent peg situated on the right side of the wagon, farthest from the barrel at the race's start.

Peg man: One of the two outriders whose job it is at the start of the race to throw in one of the two tent pegs.

Outfit: The four horses hitched to the wagon. An outfit can also include the driver, the outriders, and the outriding horses.

Outrider: One of either two or four people who, along with the driver and horses, form a chuckwagon outfit. Each outrider is responsible for performing specific tasks at the race's beginning, and for following the wagon, on horseback, to the finish line.

Pacer race: A trotting or pacing race for standard-bred horses harnessed to sulkies.

Parimutuel betting: A system of co-operative wagering in which those who have bet on the winning horses divide the total amount of money bet (less deductions for tax and racetrack commissions).

Pole: See wagon pole.

Pony chariot races, and pony chuckwagon races: Pony chariot races feature two horses pulling a light chariot. Four horses pull the lighter chuckwagons. Generally, no outriders are featured. The races are held mainly in the provinces of British Columbia, Alberta, Saskatchewan, and Manitoba. In B.C. only, there are three height classes: fifty inches, fifty-two inches, and fifty-four inches; elsewhere, pony horses used must be no taller than fifty-four inches measured at the withers. Many of the "ponies" possess thoroughbred blood.

Rangeland Derby: The Calgary Stampede's Rangeland Derby pulls together thirty-six chuckwagon cowboys, including the four Stampede finalists from the previous year, as well as the previous year's top sixteen drivers from both the World Professional Chuckwagon Association and the Canadian Professional Chuckwagon Association. It runs for ten days, usually starting the first Friday in July.

Reach: The six-by-two-inch beam joining the wagon's two axles.

Roughstock: The rodeo events that include saddle bronc riding, bull riding, and bareback riding.

Short barrel: Either Barrel 4 or Barrel 3, depending upon whether the race is amongst four chuckwagons or three chuckwagons. It is the outside starting barrel position. On the short barrel, the distance between the two barrels making up the figure-eight turn is the least.

Singletree, or whiffletree: A two-foot-long piece of wood or metal, pivoted in the middle. The horse's tugs are attached to both ends of the singletree, and the singletree's pivot point is attached to the end of the doubletree.

Skinner: A person who drives draft animals, such as mules or horses.

Stay chains: Chains that are fastened to the back of the wheel team's doubletree and lead to the wagon's axle. They allow the swivelling doubletree to swing only so far, so that if one of the horses starts, he pulls the whole wagon, and not his partner horse back.

Stove: Thrown by an outrider into the wagon's stove rack at the start, the stove was originally a heavy ranch stove. It was changed to a metal replica, and then a wooden one. It is now a light rubber imitation.

Stove up: Describes a cowboy or horse who is too old or too injured to ride.

Stretch the blanket: Tell a tall tale.

Tarp: See canvas.

Team: Two or more horses harnessed together to draw a wagon, plough, sled, etc.

Teamster: A person who drives a team (or a truck) for hauling, or racing — often as an occupation.

Tent peg, or tent pole: A five-and-one-half-foot-long wooden or metal pole. Two tent pegs — the barrel peg and the off-barrel peg — pull out and support the wagon's rear tent tarp. The tent pegs are tossed into the wagon by outriders at the race's start.

Tongue: See wagon pole.

Tonsil varnish: Whiskey.

Traces, or tugs: Strong leather straps connecting the horse's hames to a singletree. They carry the bulk of the stress from the horse pulling the wagon. If the tugs are not tight at the race's start, they can break as the horse lunges forward.

Wagon pole, pole, or tongue: The long wooden or metal shaft attached to the wagon's front axle. The pole connects to the doubletrees and neck yolks.

Wheeler: One of the rear pair of the four-horse team.

Whiffletree: See singletree.

Whistle berries: Beans.

BIBLIOGRAPHY

Belanger, Art. *Chuckwagon Racing . . . Calgary Stampede's Half Mile of Hell!* Surrey, B.C.: Heritage House Publishing Co. Ltd., 1983.

The Calgary Herald

The Calgary Sun

David, Ron. *"Chuckwagon Prayer."* In the World Professional Chuckwagon Association awards banquet program, 1999.

Fidler, Vera. *Chuckwagon of the Circle B.* Toronto: The Macmillan Company of Canada Ltd., 1957.

The Globe and Mail

Gray, James. *A Brand of Its Own.* Saskatoon: Western Producer Prairie Books, 1985.

James, Jean. *Orville: An Inside Look at Rodeo and Chuckwagon Racing.* Hanna: Gorman and Gorman Ltd., 1992.

Kennedy, Fred. *The Calgary Stampede Story.* Calgary: T. Edwards Thonger, 1952.

Livingstone, Donna. *Cowboy Spirit: Guy Weadick and the Calgary Stampede.* Vancouver: Greystone Books, 1996.

MacEwan, Grant. *Wildhorse Jack.* Saskatoon: Western Producer Prairie Books, 1983.

The National Post

Nelson, Doug. *Hotcakes to High Stakes: The Chuckwagon Story.* Calgary: Detselig Enterprises Ltd., 1993.

Savitt, Sam. *Rodeo: Cowboys, Bulls and Broncos.* New York: The Redwing Publishers, 1963.

Slatta, Richard W. *The Cowboy Encyclopedia.* New York: W.W. Norton & Company, 1994.

For more information on chuckwagons and racing dates, contact:

Canadian Professional Chuckwagon Association
Box 2411
Lloydminster, AB/SK
Canada S9V 1W5

Ph. (780) 875-2268
Fax. (780) 875-2271
www.cpcaracing.com

World Professional Chuckwagon Association
145 — 200 Rivercrest Dr. SE
Calgary, AB
Canada T2C 2X5

Ph. (403) 236-2466
Fax. (403) 279-2247
www.wpca.com